Dear
Auntie
Beeb

Dear Auntie Beeb

Sam Hare

ATHENA PRESS
LONDON

ISBN 978 1 84748 431 4

First published 2009 by
ATHENA PRESS
Queen's House, 2 Holly Road
Twickenham TW1 4EG
United Kingdom

Printed for Athena Press

Foreword

The author has been a regular listener to the World Service of the BBC for some fifty years. Today it is difficult to remember just how it used to be, or even if that was what it was called. Again, when the FM 'Far Eastern Relay Station of the BBC' for the British Forces in Singapore began exactly is in the distant past but possibly from 1960. Perhaps this was listened to because of the better reception and programmes. The rest might very well have been not very good short-wave reception. 'Singapore Broadcasting' itself did at the time produce some excellent programmes in what it called its Third Programme.

The FM station of the World Service began as the British Forces began to leave and certain members of the government here insisted that the station should remain open so that correct news bulletins could be heard. The letters here presented clearly illustrate from that time the downward deterioration of the programmes presented by the World Service. There was no political bias in those early days. There was quite a lot of real music, the sort that is still taught in schools and academies with recognised instruments, and fills the concert halls of the world.

As the former pronunciation of English deteriorated with the absence of education in English schools so the BBC had to depend more on speakers from the Commonwealth who mostly spoke clear English without a vulgar accent. There were alien influences from various minority groups professing their individual lines, with a lot of shouting and of dirty words too. The Liberal Loony Left obviously had some influence and plays had to be 'disturbing' and we all had to be 'challenged'. This author could not see why. There were enough challenges in everyday life. These letters then began with a modicum of praise and as the reader will see the writer's attitude slowly changed to one of criticism. The letters were not written really with any view to publication. They just filled a file that was about to be shredded.

BBC *Write-On*
Bush House
London

4 April 1988

Dear Sirs

Just who do you reckon listens to all those irritating *Multi-Track* programmes? Our morons and noodleheads are either on the school bus or should be in bed. This twanging and banging is very infantile and more suited to decadent European audiences than the ears of the upwardly mobile South-East Asian. Can't you shift these programmes off the peak listening hours?

Yours etc.

Sam Hare

BBC *Write-On*
Bush House
London

4 April 1988

Dear Sirs

Why do we have broadcast a weekly serial (the *Citizens*) and repetitions of it, and other plays in provincial accents, when we are reliably informed by you that, of the twenty-five to thirty million world service listeners, only a small per cent speak English? Liverpudlian, Sauchiehall Street and Gwent are little-understood dialects of English so why broadcast them to all those listeners in the world who you know very well do not have English as their second, third or even fourth language? What message for the world are those dismal sounds supposed to have? Accented English is pleasant with a good speaking voice, but in those contexts they are neither amusing nor decorative. One wonders if your left hand knows what the right one is doing. Does anyone care? Is there no liaison or control between the ones who knoweth and the ones who doeth?

Yours etc.

Sam Hare

BBC *Write-On* (Right On)
Bush House
London

29 May 1989

Dear Sirs

The BBC World Service Newsreel programme is not necessary.

Listeners have complained before of too many news bulletins and then comes this illuminated script with music.

The news items are usually pretty ghastly and horrific, with lots of deaths, earthquakes and disappearances at sea, so why trivialise with ornamental Toytown tunes? The spoken comment is rather fast for Third World listening and too camp. For instance, when Mr Takeshita's political aide committed suicide – it was a sudden last item of news – the Voice remarked, 'Well, he'll take his secrets to his grave, won't he!' followed, it seemed, by some jolly plinkety-plonk flourish on the BBC electronic organ. It was like something from *Round the Horne*.

Yours faithfully

Sam Hare

BBC *Write-On* (Right On)
Bush House
London

29 May 1989

Dear Sirs

One prefers the World Service and its austerity programmes when the BBC is on strike. That programme
called *Grief* came over as sheer comedy. If it was not meant
to be so and was being played straight by people who
should have seen a psychiatrist or a parson, then the producer must be very bent. There probably are too many
people at Broadcasting House.

Yours faithfully

Sam Hare

Write-On
BBC World Service
Bush House
London

15 April 1991

Dear *Write-On*

BBC Research will tell World Service when to broadcast what programme to which group of listeners in the world. It is then possible the main listening audience now is very young and immature and not even in this very populous segment of the world at all (Japan to Bangkok). It is certainly not an adult programme that is beamed this way at peak times. Those teenage broadcasts – the many *Multi-Tracks*, Sarah Ward and *Megamix* – seem anchored for ever. They are never moved. They have so little wit or content it is always a sure signal to switch off. But the talks, more serious plays and discussions, the real music, are pushed into slots one only comes across by accident. The optimum listening times are given over to the younger group. Is this move the policy of the Foreign Office, the one who 'pays the piper?'

Yours faithfully

Sam Hare

Write-On
BBC World Service
Bush House
London

15 April 1991

Dear *Write-On*

If the average age of the world audiences is getting older, why do we have so many teenage and 'pre-teeny' programmes at peak listening times? Can't the oldies have more of their fair share? Please be more grown-up and adult, so out with *Megamix* and all *Multi-Tracks* and Sarah Ward only at the full moon.

Yours faithfully

Sam Hare

Attention! Mr John Tusa, Paddy Feeny, Archbishop Tutu, Oliver Seer at the BBC[1], Trevor Huddleston and the Chief Rabbi

Write-On
BBC World Service
Bush House
London

15 April 1991

Dear *Write-On*

BBC World Service surely aims to reach the maximum listening audience it can and broadcast its best programmes, super radio plays, snippets of British culture, criticism, scientific and technological notes, interspersed with accurate news bulletins, etc., etc., at times best suited to those maximum audiences. It is funded by the Foreign Office.

It would seem there is a best listening time for the two hours before midnight GMT for a vast audience from Japan to Bangkok, taking in Hong Kong, China, Taiwan, Philippines, Malaysia and Singapore. At the same time, on the other side of the world it is cocktail and bath-time in the West Indies, New York and Caracas. Admittedly there may be other listeners in the world but that period mentioned will take in a fair number of the bright ones, and is the area to be most influenced.

---

[1] Oliver Seer is not a person's name. It is the sound of one. It came at the end of any programme presented by one Oliver Scott, who would sound off at the end with 'and it is bye from me Oliver Scott and all-of-us-'ere at the BBC. Thank you for listening!' 'All-of-us-'ere' of course sounded just like 'Oliver Seer'!

Why then do we in this area get hived off with some strangely juvenile programmes at these 'peak' listening hours and with few of the familiar 'oldies for adults'? It is fast becoming like the old *Children's Hour*.

For instance, *Counterpoint* is a new and stimulating programme with new sounds. No matter that it hits the ears at wake-up time (our 06.30) in Singapore. It is new and interesting. But since 1 April some old familiar programmes seem to have been moved and un-slotted. One can understand the Financial Report has to move because, with your summertime, the London Market closes later on GMT. But why do others move?

Certainly you have to design programmes towards certain bands of listeners round the world, rather than for the convenience of the announcer's breakfast and teatimes, i.e. for those listeners who are just getting up, or taking evening baths or going to bed. These would be the optimum times for a maximum listening audience, wherever.

So, at 22.30 GMT you are waking us up in the Far East. (Yet at 22.20 GMT you have already started your Financial Report!) Japan and Sydney have been awake for an hour, but Indonesia and Thailand have yet to wake. After midnight-thirty GMT it is always difficult here to pick up World Service outside the range of Singapore's FM station, for instance in Kelantan in Malaysia, because of the morning sun, etc. Your best listening audience then moves westward with the changing dawn. Perhaps at that time you are aiming more for the mid-evening listener in Boston or Bogota? Are they listening in at that hour? You must know, by now, what are each region's best listening times in all parts of the world.

My complaint now is that we in Singapore seem to have been put in the pre-teenies' listening slot, which is unsuited to the brisk outgoing yuppie import-export merchant type you are busy waking up before midnight GMT. To attract them away from the quite good local FM station your programmes will have to be slicker.

Our best listening times are probably 23.00 to midnight GMT and then again from 10.30 to 11.30 GMT. And that will go for the uncounted millions in the area outlined in Paragraph 2. But because these are our 'best times' we have to suffer that silly *Megamix*, a sure switch-off signal. It is too childish and throughout displays such ignorance, imbecility, and poor taste. Is 'Wot's up, Doc!' the way to introduce a doctor? Very often he is a consultant of some years' standing and surely not undeserving of some respect? Is it nice? In the Third World, where most of your listeners live, a doctor is still a very respected person. He is not, as in England, a Mr Bumble, a ridiculed figure of fun and disrespect. Then *Multi-Tracks* One, Two and Three and Sarah Ward on Saturday mornings here play too much junk sound; some tunes are twenty and thirty years old and were not much good when new. For whose little ears are these noises?

Now, those programmes never get moved forward or backward, which convinces me we are in the teenagers' listening slot. Are the teeny-boppers of Bogota so important at that time? It's midday in Fiji and New Zealand so they will have gone to sleep again. And it's bath-time in Bermuda. Just who are you aiming at? (At whom are you aiming?)

No longer are we encouraged to enjoy *Brain of Britain* or *Just a Minute* unless one listens in the middle of the night or during office hours. Who is listening in? Mauritius and Baghdad? Lima and Los Angeles? I am not. But I used to hear them regularly year in year out without any fiddling. These programmes were always there.

Twice a week it seems the BBC puts out some nice music (*Composer of the Week* and Richard Baker) when I am able to listen. You will be able to quote from your *Radio Times* that actually we are inundated with sonatas, symphonies and sopranos from Monday to Sunday. But I am not then switched on. Anyway, the rest of the time it is nothing but that precocious banging and twanging that a child will do when cross, and why you think this is programme music for teeny-boppers in Middle Africa I cannot think. They have so much better music of their own that they must be quite amused at those 'Strüwelpeters' on the drums.

Of course all this noise has its use. One knows it's the BBC by the sound of all that thrumming and drumming. The News will surely come, as night follows day, and there will be a talk on Hinduism or Islam, on rape, forgiveness, child abuse, shame (grief was sheer comedy) or guilt. Who slips in these Liberal topics? Mrs Dutt-Pauker of Hampstead?[2] People who delight in such despair should go back to their analyst.

It could only be the BBC.

With the warmest regards

Sam Hare

---

[2] Mrs Dutt-Pauker was a character created for an amusing and critical column in the *Daily Telegraph*. She was very left-wing and present on all parades of protest against the establishment, wherever. Her daughter Deirdre was always being pushed out of the house to 'go and protest at something'!

Write-On
BBC World Service
Bush House
London

30 April 1991

Dear *Write-On*

Positively the last letter on this matter. Your best programmes are not beamed at my best listening hours, and
that must go for a large sector of the world's listeners.

See the chart.

From 22.30 (our 6.30 a.m.) to midnight GMT (our
8 a.m.) we now find the intelligent programmes have
already begun at 22.15 GMT. So I know you do not have
us under consideration, but what about listeners further
East, maybe the Japanese or the inhabitants of Guam?

If you consider the chart you will note a band of super
listeners in the aforementioned bracket in Hong Kong,
Philippines, Malaysia and Singapore and Australia and
maybe China, and there is the opposite side of the clock on
the opposite side of the world on the Eastern seaboard of
N. America who are just changing for dinner.

Please adjust out[3] *Megamix* and the *Multi-Tracks* One,
Two and Three.

Yours faithfully

Sam Hare

---

[3] i.e. cut out.

World Service
International Audience Correspondence
British Broadcasting Corporation
Bush House
PO Box 76
Strand
London WC2B 4PH

26 May 1993

Dear Mr Hare

I am writing on behalf of the Director-General in response to your letter of 3 May, a copy of which has also been passed to us from the Broadcasting Complaints Commission.

Your comments have been read with interest by the Editor of the World Service in English, who is sorry that you find some of the output to be of low quality.

In response to your annoyance at the humour of the monthly, satirical *Two Cheers* programmes, we would argue that the inclusion of light entertainment on the network is a measure of the World Service's brief to represent life and culture in the UK. Moreover, we are probably the only international broadcaster which has such a programme, and it does serve as additional evidence for many listeners of our independence of government control.

Programmes of popular music are similarly included in the schedule as part of our reflection of life in this country. There is actually a very great demand for such programmes in various parts of the world, especially Africa and the Indian subcontinent (where the World Service in English has its largest audiences).

We hope that you will continue to tune in to the Service despite your misgivings.

With best wishes

Rupert Preston Bell

cc Director-General

Mr R D Hewlett
The Broadcasting Complaints Commission
Grosvenor Gardens House
35 & 37 Grosvenor Gardens
London SW1W 0BS

13 June 1993

Dear Mr Hewlett

Thank you for forwarding my letter to the Director-General of the World Service. I was not to know that complaints must fall into a specific category. Who would? It will narrow down your work to essentials.

Just for interest I am enclosing my reply to the letter sent on behalf of the Director-General. It seems to excuse the low quality of its light entertainment on the grounds that the millions of their listeners in Africa and India appreciate it. Which is not surprising.

But I question their not playing the National Anthem after the Queen's speech to her armies in the Gulf War. Also their noted propagation of Saddam's news bulletins *vis-à-vis* ours as though they had equal validity. Then on Armistice Sunday they filled the moment of the two minutes' silence with an advertisement for their radio magazine!

Yours sincerely

Sam Hare

P.S. Why, on the occasion of H M Queen's birthday, should the World Service decide to air its views on monarchy? It airs the popular and erroneous view of H M being a burden on the taxpayer. In 1992 (latest figures in

Whitaker 1993 – p.300)[4] the Queen's income was £113 million and £70 million of that was just paid into the Exchequer, as 'surplus revenue'. But no one tells the taxpayer that bit. The Royal Train does not come into it. This should be provided without a grumble by British Rail, who inherited the tradition from the old private railway companies of gladly supplying for free a Royal Train on every occasion. Now they can't even run it on time.

Why, on the occasion of H M Queen's recent visit to Northern Ireland, did the BBC choose to announce that 'this was *only* the *third* visit of the Queen to Northern Ireland in the whole *forty* years of her reign'. Why the stress on these words? The tone was totally pejorative and unnecessary.

---

[4] In the latest edition of *Whitaker's Almanack 2007* the Crown Estate was given as worth more than £5 billion. No doubt, as in the past, two thirds of its carefully saved income or more would be freely given to the Treasury then to be further squandered by the profligate Chancellor of the Exchequer. Whoever.

World Service
International Audience Correspondence
British Broadcasting Corporation
Bush House
PO Box 76
Strand
London WC2B 4PH

3 March 1995

Dear Mr Hare

Thank you for your latest letter addressed to the Director-General, BBC World Service and *Write-On*. I understand that your letter was featured in the programme recently and very much hope you were able to listen to the edition concerned.

As you will be aware, the new World Service schedules will come into effect on 1 April this year. These schedules have been tailored to the different regions of the world and you should find many of your favourite programmes, including music, are now on the air at times which suit you better. I am enclosing the new programme guide which gives full details of the schedules and the best frequencies for your part of the world.

As the guide shows, you will soon be able to listen to *Composer of the Month* on Saturdays at 1330 hours (repeated on Mondays at 1030 hours and Wednesdays at 0515 hours), *The Greenfield Collection*[5] on Sundays at 1600 hours and *Concert Hall* on Sundays at 2215 hours (repeated on Tuesdays at 1600 hours). All the times I have given here

---

[5] Edward Greenfield had a vast collection of recorded music and it was a delight to listen to his choice of them. But he was not to the taste of the BBC World Service and he was brushed aside. No more real music. Back to 'teeny-bops' and 'boom-boom'.

are Singapore times and I hope you will find them convenient.

Thank you again for writing and please do keep listening. I hope the information I have provided proves useful.

Yours sincerely

J Allen

Enc. programme guide

The BBC World Service Magazine
Worldwide
Bush House
PO Box 76
Strand
London WC2B 4PH

5 March 1995

Dear Mr Hare

Thank you for your letter dated 23 January concerning listening in South-East Asia. Due to a shortage of space on the Letters page we have been unable to publish it, but I enclose a reply we have received from Elizabeth Wright, Head of Region, Asia-Pacific.

Yours sincerely

Diane Cross
Features Sub-Editor, BBC Worldwide

Dear Mr Hare

Thank you for your letter of 23 January.

I am very sorry that you find not only some of our programmes, but the times at which they are scheduled, unsuitable. I am afraid that the problem lies with the fact that until now we have had only one stream of English programming to suit listeners all around the world. Inevitably, if the schedule suits listeners in, for example, Athens, it may well not suit listeners who are tuning in at quite a different time in another part of the world. The same applies to the type of programmes. Because we have listeners all over the world, of a broad age-range and varied interests, what pleases one will not necessarily please another.

However, I both hope and expect that from 1 April part of the problem should be ameliorated. We will be broadcasting five English streams, with programmes scheduled to suit the daily habits of our listeners in different geographical areas. At peak listening times in the morning and evening, when audience research tells us that people want to hear news and current affairs, that is what we will provide. Pop music and programmes for the young will be at times when we think that THEY will be listening. And I hope that the programmes which you enjoy will be at times which you find convenient.

The basic programme mix remains more or less the same, as a broad listenership needs a broad range of programmes. We have retained a large number of the old favourites, as well as commissioning some new programmes and series which I hope you will find interesting, thought provoking and even entertaining!

Yours sincerely

Elizabeth Wright
Head of Region, Asia-Pacific

BBC World Service
From the Managing Director
British Broadcasting Corporation
Bush House
PO Box 76
Strand
London
WC2B 4PH

22 March 1995

Dear Mr Hare

Thank you for your recent letter about the timing of World
Service programmes and for the copies of your previous
correspondence.

On 1 April, we shall be replacing our current single
stream of English programmes which is broadcast simul-
taneously to all parts of the world with five streams, each
directed to a different area. The programmes will be the
same for everyone, but we shall be able to arrange them to
suit the needs of particular time zones better than we can at
the moment.

I am enclosing a copy of the schedule for your area.
You will see that there is a concentration on news and
current affairs in your 'breakfast' slot as research
suggests that this is what most people want to start their
day.

Your evening slot includes both the week's main
classical music feature and the quiz as well as drama, arts
programmes and documentaries. Edward Greenfield is on
Sunday afternoon and *Concert Hall* has moved an hour
earlier on Sunday evening which should make it more
accessible for listeners in Singapore.

I am afraid that *Music Review* remains on Friday afternoon, but I hope that you find the new arrangements generally serve you better.

Yours sincerely

Sam Younger

Quote/Unquote
BBC World Service
PO Box 76
Strand
London WC2B 4PH

24 March 1995

Dear Sirs

Two more quotes which I cannot find the origin of.
Maybe you can?

1. 'America is the only Nation/Country which has pro-
    gressed from the primitive state to a condition of
    decadence without any period of civilisation/civilising
    influence in between.'
        I have a feeling this was the French statesman,
    (there weren't many) called Monet, in the fifties. It
    was not Churchill or Shaw or Wilde.

2. 'The show ain't over till the fat lady sings.'
        I tried William Safire on this and he replied he was
    'too busy'.
        It could be W C Fields, Schnozzle Durante,
    Groucho Marx, Damon Runyon or Thurber. I doubt
    if it was Humphrey Bogart.[6]

Provided your programmes are not too disrupted after
1 April I might hear this in my bath on a Thursday night or
else at 7.30 a.m. local time on Fridays. The quotes are
approximations.

Yours faithfully

Sam Hare

---

[6] The first three names were well-known Hollywood actors of the twenties and thirties.
The last two writers for *The New Yorker*. Bogart came on in the forties and fifties.

Write-On
BBC World Service
PO Box 76
Bush House
Strand
London WC2B 4PH

27 March 1995

Dear *Write-On*

You did ask us to write in!

The 9.00–9.30 Sunday morning programme of 'vargas', i.e. Indian music (Singapore Time) is not funny any more. Then *South Asia News* follows which has nothing to do with Singapore.

You might lump Bangladesh, maybe Burma, in your South Asia band of programmes, but NOT anyone further east. We have nothing in common. The influence, culture and languages are South-EAST Asian, i.e. Thai, Indonesian and Malay, and South China. Even the Tagalog language of the Philippines is closely related to Malay, and ALL aim to speak English properly if they don't already do so.

Please put your Indian music and funny accents (they are funny to us in South-East Asia) on your Indian language broadcasts. News about Karachi, Lahore, Delhi and Dakar should surely only appear if relevant on a general BBC news bulletin. Madras and Calcutta too. It is surely presumptuous that the BBC puts out an Indian pro-gramme. We know you are clever and can, but listeners in South Asia can hear enough of that already, day in day out, from their own stations. The limited time available should surely be relaying BRITISH noises. That's what the local people will expect to hear, not, 'And now let us hear Teeni Fergina singing her favourite varga with Bumi Gumi on the harmonium,' etc., etc.

I don't know how you are going to organise your new programmes but whichever way they should have a BRITISH sound, and one that is easily understood, i.e. without that heavy regional accent. To present programmes deliberately in the 'vulgar tongue' as though you hadn't got anyone left who can speak the language properly is surely an insult to the listener. It is as though you have a vested interest in being 'common'. How to correct all those mispronunciations? There is the Northerner who can't help himself saying ONE rhyming with 'DON' instead of 'DUN', and you make him read out the football results interminably. I think reference to Fowler's *Modern English Usage* could help in the pronunciation and emphasis of some of the longer words like 'contribute' and 'distribute' and 'controversy'. You used to be very good and correct.

We'll see what 1 April brings.

Yours faithfully

Sam Hare

Elizabeth Wright
Head of Region, Asia-Pacific
Bush House
PO Box 76
London

28 March 1995

Dear Elizabeth Wright

Thank you. I have been studying your new brochure of South-East Asian programmes.

It should be much less irritating. *Megamix* and the many *Multi-Tracks* have been shunted away, to India and Pakistan. Thank you. I hope they enjoy!

Now shouldn't your *In Praise of God* programmes really reflect the officially accepted religion of Britain, which is the Anglican Church? We know it is not very well attended and is probably breaking up but the BBC needn't give that impression. What about straightforward 'no nonsense' old-fashioned services, Matins or Evensong, from our great cathedrals? You need not be in the business of furthering the break-up of the Church of England. Just play it as it is without pandering to the fringe minorities, some of whom are not even Christian. The BBC ought not to be propagating Islam, Judaism or Hinduism. Those can be treated as 'interest subjects' separately in some of your talks. So very often you seem to mock and put on some multi-noodlehead assembly from Cardiff Docks. That is only belittling (pejorative) and poking fun. It does not set a good example to the world listener. They are still 'Believers'.

The old *Daily Prayer* has been replaced by *Words of Faith*. I hope this remains part of the Christian teaching too. The BBC has no business plugging other religions at all. It is not expected. Whatever the multiracialists might feel, the other religions are still very thin on the ground and Britain has not yet been taken over by Islam or Hinduism. We can then still pretend we are a Christian country. The BBC is still British, just.

Is Oliver Scott becoming Devil's Advocate or Mrs Mandela's? Moral Philosophy teaches that 'the end does not justify the means'. In this century alone surely there is proof enough of that. Winnie Mandela has used any means to achieve her object and these should not be concealed under some 'do-gooder' blanket. The BBC should not be seen to be trying to condone evil. Only fair and good means will ever achieve a fair and good end, though often not quite what was intended. (This morning's News.)

Yours sincerely

Sam Hare

The Editor
The Economist
25 St James's Street
London SW1A 1HG

3 April 1995

Dear Sir

In *Backing Britain* (01-04-95) Alastair Goodlad could be misled. Though his Ministry pays the money, the BBC World Service generally projects BBC views. They are often not very British, and have been quite anti-British.* This bias derives from the Manchester-Irish staff recruited seemingly through the columns of the Leftish *Guardian* newspaper. Otherwise, Mr Goodlad has, as usual, got it all right.

Yours faithfully

Sam Hare

*1. Deliberately omitting the playing of the National Anthem after Her Majesty the Queen's speech to her army in the Gulf War.

*2. The Two Minutes' Silence here on one Armistice Day being filled with their advertisement, and jingle, for their radio magazine.

*3. At the ceasefire in Northern Ireland, the BBC sent a demand letter signed by eight or twelve 'fellow-travellers or sleepers', asking for the immediate release from prison of all the convicted IRA thugs.

  'BRITAIN' represents ALL the kingdoms, Wales, Ireland, Scotland and England, so organisations purporting to be British should not express partisan feelings.

Sam Younger
Bush House
PO Box 76
The Strand
London WC2B 4PH

4 April 1995

Dear Sam Younger

So far so good. Your changes on the World Service are apparent and palpable.

Selfishly speaking, and also for others perhaps in the (+8 GMT) sector, I am sure Japan (+9 GMT) might appreciate more the *BBC English* programme and exchange this with the slot an hour before, at 21.15 GMT, which includes at the moment your quiz programme and two periods of decent music. These appear at, Singapore Time, a quarter past five in the morning. Most people aren't awake.

Understanding fully that you can't please all the people all of the time, I wish you luck.

Of course we are very fortunate here in Singapore in inheriting the former Forces Broadcasting Station and have FM reception. It is very difficult further north in Malaysia, out of reach of the FM station. Reception of short wave is not very good even during the hours of darkness. I shall try again now I have the frequencies listed clearly. I go to Kelantan next month.

The *BBC English* programme is interesting, but I think it is going to irritate if I have to hear it every day except Sundays. I would much rather hear some decent music, and the quiz.

With best regards

Sam Hare

Mr Sam Younger
BBC World Service
Bush House
PO Box 76
Strand
London

8 April 1995

Dear Sam Younger

The general impression of your new programme is good. It sounds more adult in presentation. The short fifteen minute bits and pieces I have been able to hear are interesting and amusing.

This morning's *Music Making* was pleasant and informative. The sound of the contra-flute I have never heard before that I can remember, unless it occurs in *Peter and the Wolf* or Britten's *Young Person's Guide to the Orchestra*. The serpent and anaconda I know but haven't heard for some time since my friend Christopher Monk, who made both and played them, has died. In Edwardian morning dress he led a consort of serpents to open a football match in America, which must have shaken them somewhat, being used to the usual cheerleaders and pom-pom dancers.

Now is too much time being wasted in introducing 'Future Attractions'? There are snippets of music and announcements, often cut short by some joker on the switchboard. Have someone play the tape back and check. This has occurred at least twice. Announcers, on tape, being cut short in mid-flow. Do we really need such formality in announcing what is to come shortly?

How about a new relay station in South Thailand? It might cover the top end of Malaya, Thailand and

Cambodia and South Vietnam. The latter countries now have a preference for English over French.

Now how about exchanging that fifteen minute slot at 21.15 (GMT) with the one at 22.30 (GMT)? I am sure the Japanese would prefer *BBC English*! It is always interesting but I would prefer to be hearing your music.

Thank you anyway.

With best regards

Sam Hare

Write-On
BBC World Service
Bush House
Strand
London WC2

21 April 1995

BBC World Service Changes Etc.

Dear *Write-On*

On the whole there is improvement because some adolescent programmes have moved away from my listening slot.

As I have said, often, it is difficult for you to please everyone all the time, but I reckon there are few people able to listen all day long. Each sector of the world will have its prime-time listening slot. The South-East Asian one with China, Mongolia, Yakutia, Indonesia, Burma, Thailand and Philippines is a big one.

The BBC English item is new to us and is interesting though I'd rather swap it with the *Composer of the Month* half-hour. But why use American accents? That must be a little nasty BBC joke! And it is unnecessary. The American language is usually slurred, and their consonants FKPS and T are mispronounced to become respectively VGBZ and D. It is a lazy form of speech and is not to be copied just because some people assume it to be 'cool'. (Take that Mark Steyn for instance!)

Two new features are not 'World Service Quality' and should go back to your provincial light programmes where they might be better understood. There is that quiz about stage or radio shows with its accompaniment of coarse, shrieking laughter. With the disturbed reception in many areas this will be little understood and can have no purpose. It could be replaced with a more adult general knowledge quiz.

The second one is also a quiz about sports personalities. How this can be of interest to the people of North Thailand or Mindanao or Outer Mongolia and Inner Africa can only be imagined. Of none I would think. Return it to the provincial light programmes whence it came. Few will understand what it is about. And it includes someone's raucous hyena-like laugh – is it from nervousness? – that goes 'YE-EAH-YAK-YAK-YAK-HEH!' when anyone says anything at all. It is all a light-weight item only of interest to light-weight folk at home with a passive interest in sports.

Please check on the editing of your tapes and discs of recorded voices. There is some announcer whose identity is daily being cut short at the first letter 'E—'. We shall never know if he is Edward, Edwin, Edmond, Edgardo, Ethelred, Egbert, Eric, Et, Evan or Ezra.

I still haven't heard much music; a little morning Schubert only. Last Sunday afternoon I was in Kuala Lumpur where the awful reception of the World Service is notorious. Maybe you could persuade the Malaysian Government to use one of those twin towers they are building as the highest in the world, to hold one BBC transmitter. They have become suddenly interested in teaching English after twenty-five years. They threw out your old station at Masai in Johor.

For your interest and delectation I am including a bundle of letters written to various and sundry from John Birt to Sam Younger, Elizabeth Wright, Nellie Dean *et alia*.

One last thing: I see you are broadcasting *The Chronicles of Clovis* on your Home Programmes. Can't we have that in place of some of the drivel you put out? These and any Wodehouse, which you are particularly good at, would be great fun, and popular in India and Japan for that matter. And some Christmas you could repeat that *Get Santa* play. There is no need to put on plays that face up to problems. These are YOUR PROBLEMS, not ours, and we are not interested in your inability to solve them by shouting about them.

I don't write all this guff hoping that a letter will be read out. I write so that you will understand we appreciate the more adult programmes and that you might be able to change a few things, and find me some music!

Yours faithfully

Sam Hare

Write-On
BBC World Service
Bush House
Strand
London WC2

27 April 1995

Dear *Write-On*

Very many thank yous for the change of programmes.

A year or so ago we began to lose our music programmes by some switching to suit somebody. Edward Greenfield moved away and then there was another half-hour of requests for 'proper' music. One could never hear a whole symphony or an opera, but one got snatches, which were always welcome. Then for a year or more in my listening slot, anyway, we got nothing, except by accidental listening at some odd hour.

Let us hope for more than is on offer at the moment.

Thank you for moving the *Multi-Tracks* One, Two and Three. They just spelt noise and irritation.

Thank you for shifting Gavin Claxton also. I managed to get him four times a week by some misfortune, usually in the bath. Not very funny. I am sure he wears a baseball cap back to front and his shirt out, so trendy, like Princess Di. His catchphrase 'Ehh, what's up, doc?'[7] seemed to be mostly concerned with teenagers' 'piles, pimples and periods'. It was not a very intelligent programme and perhaps it was designed to be just that, to attract the

---

[7] This was a signature greeting of 'Bug's Bunny', the cheeky and irreverent cartoon character, from Looney Tunes of Warner Bros. interpreted as 'What is up Doc?' meaning 'How's it going Doc?' Perhaps this was the beginning of the denigration of and disrespect for the medical profession? It began in America and was transferred to Britain as the NHS deteriorated and patients and doctors exploited it.

unsettled minds of the young around the world. No doubt it has served its purpose.

You have unsympathetic and incompatible interviewers, to wit

(a) that smart-Alec super-salesman voice talking to the quietly spoken intelligent saxophonist early this week. And

(b) the insensitive young thing reading out her brief, interviewing a sensitive poet who did understand better the use of language. This week.

In the *BBC English* programme, new to us in this slot, it does seem wrong to have the American dialect spoken. In America, that is in the USA, they usually omit six of the letters in our alphabet.

The C soft S-sound so often becomes Z.

F is V; P becomes B; T is D and K becomes G and of course S is Z.

For example, in the 22.30 GMT Wednesday programme the words 'So unsophisticated' became 'Zoh un-zoh-vizz-dig-gayzded'. And 'New York' sounded like 'Nee-yoo-orrgg'. I don't think they realise how many letters they are missing and they think we have FUNNY ACCENTS. It is THEY who have the ACCENT!

And surely 'resources' is pronounced even in English with the sybillant 'S' sounds, not the 'zees...'

The BBC need never be ashamed of speaking English PROPERLY, and that does not mean 'posh'. It means pronouncing the letters and words WITHOUT an accent, no drawl, no long diphthong vowels when they should be short sounds. Whatever happened to your elocutionist? It should be remembered that most of the world is trying very hard to learn English. Most of them are intelligent enough to realise that the English spoken in England, rather than in America, is the correct form. They expect you to be of some assistance in this.

I see poor Andy Kershaw gets squeezed when the *Play of the Week* is ninety minutes long. No harm done, I fear. But it would be pleasant once or twice in the year to use such a ninety-minute slot for, say, a Bruckner symphony. Please don't fill it with one of your dramas on 'home topics that we must face up to'. These are for you in your Light Programmes to face up to. Not the world at large. Botswanaland, Malawi and Manila have enough of their own problems, and yours are to them incomprehensible. (Where does Andy Kershaw come from? Tadcaster or Doncaster?)

Thank you for listening.

Regards and, thank you, I don't want a T-shirt.

Yours faithfully

Sam Hare

Mr Sam Younger
BBC World Service

2 June 1995

Dear Sam Younger

Does anyone monitor the BBC World Service? Though it is funded by the Foreign Office, do they listen?

At 22.30 GMT 1 June, (i.e. this morning here) they broadcast such nonsense and republican propaganda disguised as an English language programme.

A voice explained that H M Queen received her income from the Civil List which therefore was taxpayers' money. And then added that no tax was paid until after the Great Fire at Windsor.

Now *Whitaker's Almanack* clearly shows each year the source and amount of the Sovereign's income which is the Crown Estate (Crown Estate Commission, Whitehall, SW1). Since 1760 the Land Revenues of England and Wales have been collected by them on behalf of the Crown, of Ireland from 1820 and Scotland since 1833. This Revenue is termed the Consolidated Fund.

The Civil List is the amount of estimated household expenditure and is taken out of that Consolidated Fund.

What remains is given to the Treasury and saves the taxpayer some millions of pounds. The revenue was from the Sovereign's properties.

There seems to be no way of countering this propaganda.

Also, in speaking of Ireland more or less at the same time, it was implied it had been under 'Colonial Rule' and ruled from London for 700 years – and would soon be free. This is garbled history. The Kingdom of Ireland was 'united' with England from the time of Henry VIII. Who writes these programmes, and who does not censor them?

I'm afraid there are too many Manchester *Guardian* Irish 'sleepers' infesting those corridors at Langham Place and Bush House.

Yours sincerely

Sam Hare

Sam Younger
Bush House
PO Box 76
The Strand
London WC2B 4PH

6 June 1995

Dear Sam Younger

1. Reception is now pretty good in the north of Malaysia, i.e. in Kota Bharu, Kelantan. Through the daytime on 6195 kHz and at night and early morning on 11955 kHz. I've just been there.

2. I approve of the new station for Thailand. Just where is it to be?

3. I disapprove of the strong republican propaganda fitted into the subject matter of the *English Language* programme this morning. That was sly and cheating. Not what that programme is for.

4. In that same programme you have American pronunciation, which is wrong if you are teaching English. For instance the correct pronunciation of 'cyclical' is with the 'ai' sound as in 'eye', 'aisle', as shown in the *Oxford English Dictionary*. Go look see. It does not have the 'ick' sound as in 'sick'.
   There are folk in the BBC who enjoy being contrary.

5. Andy Kershaw's dialect does NOT go with introducing excellent Middle African music from Zaire, Uganda or Zimbabwe or wherever else! He'd be better with brass bands.

6. What does 'newsday' mean? That is a new word. I don't see why you can't keep to the news, or news desk, or news hour.

7.   It can't have been easy but I think the new arrange-
     ment is a lot better. I still haven't heard much music
     beyond Fauré. One concert late one night, here.

Yours sincerely

Sam Hare

The Broadcasting Complaints Commission
Grosvenor Gardens House
35 & 37 Grosvenor Gardens
London SW1W 0BS

12 June 1995

Dear Mr Hare

Thank you for your letter of 6 June.

As you will see from the enclosed leaflet, the BCC is an independent statutory body which deals with complaints of unjust or unfair treatment or unwarranted infringement of privacy in or in connection with a programme, but the complaint must be from the person who has been personally affected by the unfairness or alleged infringement of privacy. I am afraid your complaint does not fall within our remit.

However, I am forwarding your letter to BBC World Service. Their address is: Bush House, London WC2B 4PH.

Yours sincerely

Robert Hargreaves
Secretary

World Service
International Audience Correspondence
British Broadcasting Corporation
Bush House
PO Box 76
Strand
London WC2B 4PH

12 June 1995

Dear Mr Hare

Thank you for writing to the BBC World Service. We apologise for the delay in replying but we are keeping careful note of audience reaction to the new schedules and appreciate the time you have taken in writing to us with your views.

When we devised the new schedules, we made every effort to try to make them appropriate for the region to which they were being broadcast, with appropriate programmes at appropriate times. However, in the case of the Asia-Pacific region we are trying to cater for a very wide spread of time difference ranging from GMT +6½ (Burma) and GMT +12 (New Zealand). Inevitably, some programmes simply will not be at convenient times as we had to take GMT +8 as the middle point.

However, we will shortly be examining the schedules with a view to making minor alterations in the Autumn. We are taking the concerns of listeners seriously and will do our best to accommodate the common issues which have been raised, although we should point out that we have had very good feedback from listeners as well as some complaints.

We do apologise for any inconvenience the new schedules have caused you, but hope you will continue to listen to the World Service.

Thank you again for writing. We enclose our current programme guide which we hope you will find useful.

Yours sincerely

J Allen

Enc. programme guide

Nicola Barringer, Sam Younger, *Write-On*, etc.
BBC World Service
Bush House
PO Box 76
The Strand
London WC2B 4PH

12 August 1995

Dear Sir/Madam

Regarding that 'Phone-in programme on Colonialism' – the voice from Sri Lanka that got cut off has got it all wrong. He talked about 'British influence on Demography in Malaysia' because they brought in so many Chinese.

Now demography is the 'study of statistics dealing with births, deaths and diseases of a people and is a branch of anthropology'. Nothing to do with immigration. And the Chinese were in the tin-mining districts of Malaya long before Stamford Raffles founded Singapore or Francis Light, Penang. They were found to be more efficient at getting at the tin ores.[8]

The practice of introducing Chinese workers to Malaya began with the Sultan of Johor, to work his Gambier Estates. This was so profitable that other states and Sultans followed suit. The British did try to control the numbers but did not prohibit the practice. They always get blamed but they did not deliberately, as implied, bring about this influx of Chinese labourers.

---

[8] The early Chinese migrants to the Malayan tin states brought with them their ancient expertise at pumping water. Joseph Needham's research in China reveals how old these methods were. Hence they were able to delve deeper and extract the tin ores profitably. The large mansions that were later built in Penang are evidence of their success.

Without them and their millionaire descendants Malaysia today would be a far less happy place.

Yours faithfully

Sam Hare

Elizabeth Wright, Head of Region, Asia-Pacific
Bush House
PO Box 76
The Strand
London WC2B 4PH

16 August 1995

BBC WORLD SERVICE

Dear Elizabeth Wright

The whole sound of the World Service has changed. Once more it has become a programme mostly full of interest and enlightenment. That switch-off button is rarely used.

The reservations that remain are minimal.

1. Timing: The peak listening time in S.E. Asia is from 20.30 to 01.00 GMT (our getting up and going to office time) and 10.30 to 11.30 GMT (the evening bath and changing time). Could we not divorce ourselves from the East Australia, New Zealand, Oceania and Pacific, Japan sector? They are a big listening band on their own, THREE HOURS away. Thank you for removing S.E. Asia from the South Asia people; those long Indian programmes of a Sunday morning were becoming a bore.

2. Pronunciation: Accented English is no problem so long as it is well enunciated. Often it is not. The lady on *Pop Science* growls. The man on *Vintage Chart Show* has marbles in his mouth and gabbles. One doubts if he is even speaking English; maybe Swahili.

    There is Minouk Suwando whose consonants are unclear. She is Japanese or Korean? I doubt if her voice is acceptable in India or Africa and other points West.

Doesn't Lyse Doucet deserve a holiday? She seems to have been in harness since and maybe before the Afghan War. She sounds always as though she has 'the bit in her mouth'. Are her teeth wired together?

Foreign-accented speakers are often used to give colour to a report from wherever. If the accent is too heavy then it becomes unintelligible. English speakers across the world have different accentuation of consonants and 'wowels'.

3. *Words of Faith* should come from the mainstream; not from the eccentric fringe. Already people are irreligious and the BBC should not be in the business of making more of a turkey out of a religious programme. Play it straight, or cut it out. What would be wrong with, say, five minutes of prayers daily? Being quite non-denominational. No need to waste time on explaining which faith was being used. Prayer is prayer in any religion. Then on a weekend, to hit as many Sundays as possible over your bands, let us hear Choral Evensong or Matins ONCE A MONTH from one or other of our great Anglican minsters or cathedrals or abbeys. But not from a tin-pan-alley guitar adventurist chapel in Cardiff Docks. That is making mock of the whole thing. Just present religion seriously, with a serious voice. Your World Service listener would appreciate this. Move the mischief-makers out. The other religions of the world should not go unrecognised but they should not be emphasised. Britain is still regarded as a Christian country, does behave basically in a Christian way, and generally obeys a Christian ethic without having to attend church or chapel.

'Fringe Christianity' should be avoided. Leave the gay/lesbian churches and the female priesthood to the tabloid newspapers. They need no encouragement from BBC World Service.

4. Music programmes have improved out of all proportion to what they had become. Many thanks! There is Torelli. There was Mahler's Eighth from the Proms and

the Oslo Philharmonic. The timing suits this listener at 14.00 GMT, which makes it Sunday bedtime here.

5. Short stories should be at a premium with having to fill in intervals between broadcasting longer programmes. Have you not in your ancient archives some recordings of A J Alan? His voice was a familiar one in the 1930s. Maybe on *Children's Hour*. His storytelling was clever. Of course they might sound boring today.

6. History programmes are an innovation, though there have been excellent series in the past on Japan and the Middle East. Perhaps we could have something on American Foreign Policy – that is if there ever has been one apart from greed and the acquiring of markets for their produce overseas. It's mostly been Coca-Colonisation; from their occupation, unwarranted, of the Philippines, Hawaii, and their war in Vietnam.

7. News presentation in the World Service has always striven to be impartial. It must remain so. But sometimes it can seem to be siding with the enemy, that is if Britain happens to be in the conflict. This attitude must be incomprehensible to most listeners abroad. In the Gulf War, the general impression was that the BBC was effectively relaying Saddam Hussein's propaganda, much to his delight and our confusion.

I hope all this doesn't add to your confusion since you must be getting many comments from one region to another. The general improvement is tremendous, and we in this band of listeners are glad to be rid of *Megamix* and the many *Multi-Tracks* and the South Indian dialogues. If you could just move the programmes that I only have a glimpse of at 05.15 GMT to 06.15 GMT, then this listener would be most grateful.

My gripes now are so minimal you could leave it all as it is!

Yours sincerely

Sam Hare

Write-On, BBC World Service

BBC World Service

Dear *Write-On*

You have changed the schedules while I have been away in London. Several times I passed Bush House and thought you were doing well, but you have wrecked it again. I thought I had written enough and put the file away. In August I said the switch-off button was rarely used. I'm afraid I'm inclined to use it now all the time.

Now I am speaking from South-East Asia which seems to have been lumped with South Asia, i.e. the Indian sub-continent. They have quite different listening times, at least three hours if not four *after* our slot, and tastes are different.

South-East Asia time zone will incorporate China and Siberia, Burma, Thailand, Malaysia, Indo-China countries, Indonesia, Philippines and Western Australia. We will all be getting up and listening within an hour of each other, and this is probably the major listening period. It is con-temporary with the Eastern Seaboard of America yet they are twelve hours behind. It is their cocktail hour, changing time and evening bath time.

So our slot has quite a large audience.

With your recent changes we have ended up with a rag-bag of little talks and *no music*. Shall we say not enough music is left to entice one to keep listening. The music won't come. And I don't mean all that wacky plink-a-plonk for morons; there's plenty of that through your twenty-four hours. I have looked through the whole week's schedule and remembering that for this area (see above) the best listening times for us are GMT 21.15–

01.15 (our morning time of 05.15–09.15 a.m.) A lot of people could be listening. Then in our evening, after office hours and bath time, GMT 10.30–12.30 being our 18.30–20.30 p.m.

There was music, and there still is but it has been moved to 01.15 in *our morning*! Other programmes have been switched or snipped at and put during our working hours. 'Greenfield Collection' appears on Sunday afternoon as usual for us but *Concert Hall* has given up some of its time to 'WRITE-ON'. And when you do choose a Composer of the Month you don't have to go for the obstruse as in Messiaen or Schonberg. They are not exactly everyone's cup of tea, and you know it. There is much else. Please try again.

Yours faithfully

Sam Hare

World Service
British Broadcasting Corporation
Bush House
PO Box 76
Strand
London WC2B 4PH

16 November 1995

Dear Mr Hare

Thank you for your letter of 18 October. I am sorry that you are still unhappy with the schedule. Perhaps it would help if I clarified how the Regions work. South-East Asia has not been lumped in the Indian Sub-Continent. It is part of the Asia-Pacific Region which does indeed include China, Burma, Thailand, Japan etc. As I think I have mentioned before the schedule is aimed at GMT+8.

We quite deliberately did not put music into the main listening hours in the mornings as audience research indicated that this was a time when people only listened for perhaps half an hour at a time and they wanted to know what had been going on in the world and the latest news and current affairs. The schedule was planned to reflect this demand. However, we are currently engaging in some more audience research in Hong Kong and will examine this particular question. If it emerges that a majority of people believe that we are too speech-based in the morning then we will review the situation. Since the majority of our broadcasting is still by short wave which is not the best medium for classical music, it is true that we do not have a great deal of it in the schedule. Obviously, in Singapore where World Service is broadcast on FM this is a matter of some regret. However, the FM stream in Singapore is an exception in the Region. We still feel that we have a good musical balance including music which we hope will appeal to people like yourself as well as music aimed at a younger audience. We believe that it is perfectly reasonable to broadcast the latter, as the vast majority of our listeners are between the ages of twenty-five and forty-five.

We are constantly refining our schedules to try to meet the majority of audience needs. But, as I am sure you will appreciate, no matter how hard we try it is impossible for us to please everybody all of the time. I do hope that you will keep listening to us.

Yours sincerely

Elizabeth Wright
Head of Region, Asia-Pacific

Write-On
BBC World Service
Bush House
London

25 March 1996

Dear Nicola Barringer

Thank you BBC World Service for Rossini, Weber, Schubert and Beethoven's Eighth Symphony last night (10.15 p.m. local time) and a repeat this 5.15 a.m. (local). When was the last time the World Service played Beethoven's Eighth? Then some *Eine Kleine Nachtmusik* this morning before Alistair Cooke.

Are you all right? This cannot be surely just because I wrote grumbly letters to Sir Christopher, Sam Younger and Elizabeth Wright?

And thank you, Nicola Barringer, for having a nice voice.

In your usual topical drama there are so many strong and strident ones that practise their tenor tones in vehement and vile abuse of their male partners, that one wonders why they ever formed a partnership in the first place. It is little wonder the sperm count has gone down; those harridans would severely diminish a salmon river.

I enclose copies of 'Mr Grouser's' letter signed by Sam Hare. It is for information only. You so often say you want to know what we are thinking. One doesn't seek either fame or notoriety, a T-shirt or even a fountain pen.

A pity this morning's music could not have come an hour later. I missed the half of it because of morning exercise outdoors.

With many thanks

Sam Hare

Mr Grouser's Letter

In August last year I was quite happy with the change in the World Service programme. The annoyances seemed to have been moved. But then by November other changes had occurred and for the worse. The whole seemed to have fragmented into little short-takes between the hourly news bulletins.

I will not complain about the hourly bulletins. They are what the World Service is for. People listen for them because their own stations and those of others are unreliable.

There are those five- and ten-minute 'fillers' and items that are best left to the visual senses, for example a programme on *Bones* and another *Portrait of an Artist*. No one has any imagination today so why broadcast a 'visual' subject?

A Secret Life of a Song went on far too long, was fatuous and you need not have bothered. This is broadcasting time being wasted. And thank you. *Megamix* has been slotted safely out of my ken.

Elizabeth Wright states that you do not deliberately put music into 'the main listening hours in the mornings' since audience research (Hong Kong) showed people only listened for half an hour. It is fairly obvious that there is no one attached to World Service who cares for serious music at all. There is at least some time between one news bulletin and the next for something other than hoppity-hop jazz of any vintage or 'Country Style' or Rock-around-the-Clock Funk Punk or what-have-you. I know you are trying to attract listeners and aiming at 'the Yoof' of the world. Are they worth having? In Hong Kong the Yoof can barely speak recognisable English when I phone their bank clerks and so on, so what the outcome will be when you keep broadcasting in Brummagem (Birmingham) and

Scouse (Liverpool) brogues is anybody's guess. Try researching in Singapore, Bangkok, Jakarta.

Elizabeth Wright then excuses your not broadcasting 'classical music' because it is put out on short wave. That is immaterial. I listened most of my life on short wave and had much enjoyment from just hearing a lot of fine music. It was a poor answer, since you broadcast the Promenade Concerts last year, and we actually heard Mahler's Eighth Symphony, which is always a great moment. Your programmers would not understand that.

What happened to that excellent series one of which was *Listening with Kay*? It was re-broadcast so one might hear it twice or parts of it. *My Music* has just reappeared in my orbit and that is a joy.

I do think of others in the world and that my late-night listening is someone else's getting-up time. In Singapore we are in the middle of a very populous and intelligent area which includes Burma and much of Bengal and Bangladesh, Indonesia, Thailand and Malaysia, the Philippines, Hong Kong, Taiwan and China, and Australia in its Western part. I put Japan and the Pacific a couple of hours or more earlier. They will be well into work when we are just getting up.

There seem to be rather too many snippets of 'forthcoming attractions'. They are sort of stringers or trailers of future dramas and so on, coming in an hour's time or so. Since one's listening time is necessarily short during a working week, these feelers are rather useless. One is not going to be able to hear them, so the time is wasted. The best use of little time must always be a consideration, though what one hears today seems to be, 'How can we fill in the time between our news bulletins?' And so you put in one or two sports bulletins and a lot of five-and ten-minute fillers from wherever. One wonders from which other Light Programme or Programme 3 or 4 or 5 you have borrowed. Many seem quite unsuited to a World Service whose listeners must vary from the Thai student to Muslim Indonesian. What they make of your screaming dramas filled with uncouth and violent language I do not know. Quite a lot of these home-produced 'topical productions' seem designed merely and purposely as vehicles for someone to scream vile sentences. One play that involved birdwatching somehow found itself a situation where the lady-(sic) of the plot was able to scream abuse across the Norfolk fens, at her husband.

One understands this idea that audiences 'must be challenged' but that is an idea more appropriate to a home audience where the listeners are fairly homogeneous. It is too soon to be challenging World Service listeners. With all those dirty words and screaming women and unusual situations of domesticity you might frighten them all away. They are not attractive programmes, and the problems you are trying to face up to are yours and not applicable to anywhere else in the world. People are much better behaved and better mannered in the Third World. As has been said by others, they have a 'different set of values'. They have also been a society for many thousands of years before Europeans even began to scratch each other's eyes out.

You almost give equal treatment, with news bulletins, to sports reports. Now many news bulletins include in their tail a resume of the day's sports results, yet within half an hour we get yet another report filled out with purple prose as though all sportsmen are poets in disguise. With so little time between one news bulletin and another, I would suggest the sports writers 'keep it short' and crisp. No need to amplify the beauty of someone's overarm bowling, or the sun setting over the distant cricket pitch. Twice a day should be sufficient for the purple prose people, and the football results say four times a day, or is that too much? Purple prose or not, it should be grammatical English that is spoken, with or without the necessary accent from whichever county has become BBC fashionable. (You have not tried Geordie yet!) For example: '...millions IS going to be spent...' (Sports report at 22.45 GMT on 8 December last, followed by '...the

Committee ARE...' both with reference to some sports complex in Yugoslavia. I suppose you have to supply the avid listener with all these lists of sports figures because he is filling in his football pool coupons. It is one way to attract an audience. Better for them if they all went out and played football themselves and severally.

The poor listener to serious music is badly done by. All that appears from hour to hour is the 'bop-bop' sound of the last thirty years' nursery music. Some listeners must feel music is old-fashioned after only four weeks. From the twelfth century up to the present time there is a wealth of fine and interesting and 'challenging' music, which does not mean that when time does allow you need not cheekily and mischievously present some little known contemporary musical work which the very great majority of listeners have no wish to hear, or even begin to understand.

It is not helpful to talk about *Concert Hour* or reduce it to *Concert Hall* or vice versa, then condense it further by intruding ten or more minutes of *Write-On* to delay its start. Then to reduce the substance of the musical presentation to a saxophone recital. This is not the nicest of musical instruments and can be put with the mouth organ or the hurdy-gurdy and accordion. We don't need challenging with this sort of music. If you played the real stuff you could not get through it all in any lifetime at the present rate of broadcasting. Just take a pin and open the music reference books by Scholes or Grove, and pick the popular composers. We don't have to have the strict classicists either, since there is a wealth of light music that is very pleasant to the ear. There is not enough space in the World Service to promote the lesser-known composer. That is the job for Third Programme managers.

What can be done, as I have suggested before, and Andy Kershaw is managing very nicely, is to seek out across the world the local talent and little bands from say the Philippines, Sumatra (round Lake Toba), Seychelles, Madagascar, Uganda, South Africa and Zaire and

Zimbabwe, the West African nations, then to Paraguay and Brazil, and the Mariachi bands of Mexico City. Their playing has so much more quality and sense of rhythm than any of those mechanical groups that just make noise and shout abuse. And you call that music.

You will tell me that I can listen to Edward Greenfield. He appears here at 4.15 p.m. on a Sunday afternoon. And that's that. Most folk are out and about, sailing, skiing, windsurfing, golfing and so on. Then there is Composer of the Month. I must thank you for Mahler, and now for Wagner. If you choose someone like Boulez or Alban Berg. I will know that you are not taking the job seriously and only do it to annoy. World Service has no room for avant-garde in music; the ground has to be first prepared by playing the early works of the great composers over and over again. You once put on a whole opera and played Beethoven quartets in a series, and Haydn symphonies as though you were interested.

You excel at radio drama, so let us use this ability with good plays. Forget those screaming, swearing, challenging themes. Keep those on the homeside Light Programmes where they belong with the four-letter-word ladies.

Your reviews of various countries are faultless. There was a series on the Middle East which quietly told the truth, and there was one on Japan which ended with a twist in the final word. These are historical records and can be repeated from time to time. When things are in better perspective there could be a series on the African countries and those of South-East Asia.

More recently the *Words of Faith* programmes have had a better presentation. It is good to hear an old familiar hymn sung well, by a good choir from church or abbey, with good organ playing, maybe an anthem too, but you don't have much time and not enough to go through a whole service. So, a good choir, an old church or cathedral, a good organist and some super church music, and that should do. With so little time available, I do not see why the World Service should proselytise for any religion other than Christianity. It surely is not expected, and there is not enough space available.

Can we try and remove the jokers and mischief-makers from the World Service? Maybe they go with the BBC. For example, eighteen months ago, when the Ceasefire was declared in Northern Ireland, a letter was published in the *Sunday Telegraph* demanding the release of all IRA members imprisoned. It was signed by about twelve BBC staff. You must be harbouring IRA sympathisers. Are they still then in favour of terrorism?

Some resident comedian who makes up jokes was being interviewed (why?) on some programme a year or two ago and he felt that it was quite all right to make fun of the Royal Family and its members, 'because they're nothing speshul'. Why this introspection as a programme?

Someone so ordered things that after H M Queen spoke to her army in the Gulf War, there was no National Anthem played. Who decided that one?

Why was the two minutes' silence Armistice Sunday filled with an advertisement for the *BBC World Service Magazine*? That was three or four years ago. Just who is in charge? Or is all this thought to be a scrumptious jape? Whoever is or was responsible should have his nose rubbed in his own dirt.

And a big welcome to Sir Christopher Bland. He has the Augean stables to clean.

Yours sincerely

Sam Hare

World Service
British Broadcasting Corporation
Bush House
PO Box 76
Strand
London WC2B 4PH

27 March 1996

Dear Mr Hare

Your letter to Sir Christopher Bland dated 14 March was passed to me as I am responsible for all programming of the World Service into the Asia-Pacific Region.

As most of your comments are to do with the music output, I have asked the Music Department to look into it. Once I have a response from them I will get back to you.

Yours sincerely

Elizabeth Wright
Head of Region, Asia-Pacific

Write-On
BBC World Service
Bush House
London

2 April 1996

Dear Nicola Barringer

One must be grateful for small mercies.

Thank you for more music on the World Service, and quite a lot on Sunday from 14.00 GMT. BUT can we CUT THE CACKLE!

There is so little time available in a World Service week we cannot afford the luxury of 'BABBLING and BLATHER'. There is far too much talk and so there is less music, except faintly in the background. It is the talking we would rather have in the background, or better, not at all.

Please keep these introductions to the barest minimum. We do not really wish to hear if a violinist changes his bowing or his thinking or his sitting position if he is playing Mozart, Schumann or Schütz, or how he even feels about it. We just want him to get on with playing something for our ears.

Your excellent interviewers and presenters I am sure would love to interview someone changing the tyre on a car, and enquire what his or her feelings were as they tightened the final nut. Would they feel any different if they were changing the tyre of a Jag or a Rolls? We don't want to know all that.

About HALF of the *Mastersingers* programme was taken up with John Steane muttering on. No doubt we will be hearing his voice for a long time yet but it is rare to hear Boris Christoff and Chaliapin.

Where's the producer?

With best regards

Sam Hare

World Service
British Broadcasting Corporation
Bush House
PO Box 76
Strand
London WC2B 4PH

10 April 1996

Dear Mr Hare

Further to my letter dated 27 March, I enclose a reply from Jenny Bild, Executive Producer, Music Department to the points made in your letter of 14 March to Sir Christopher Bland.

May I take this opportunity to thank you for your interest in the World Service.

Yours sincerely

Elizabeth Wright
Head of Region, Asia-Pacific

Enc.

A few thoughts on the music content of Sam Hare's comprehensive letter.

* *Composer of the Month* during the last year has featured composers such as Schubert, Fauré, the Madrigalists, Mahler, Corelli/Albinoni/Tartini, Bizet, Copland, Chopin, Mozart and Wagner. Plenty of variety, I hope, in terms of period, nationality, type etc. and plenty of tunes. The only composer who might be considered 'challenging' was Bartók, and we felt that we should not allow the 50th anniversary of his death to pass without taking the opportunity to present the life and music of a composer (who is now considered to be one of the greatest of this century) in an informative and accessible way.

  At no time would we ever consider featuring one of the avant-garde composers in this slot – as Mr Hare says, we feel them to be unsuitable for the majority of our audience, although that would not preclude talking about them in other programmes and playing short extracts for illustration.

* To 'cheekily and mischievously present some little-known contemporary musical work'. Let me assure him that every item of music played is there for a reason (we're not in the business of 'that was… and now for something completely different', nor do we feel it appropriate to produce a stream of 'light music that is very pleasant to the ear' by the popular composers – that's the business of specialised local radio stations). In order to fit into the context of the rest of World Service's output our programmes must inform as well as entertain, be 'about' music as well as 'of music' and must, above all, broaden the horizons of our listeners and reflect the diversity of the musical scene throughout the world. In this context, we feel that the music of our own times deserves to be taken seriously and treated with respect (after all, some of it

will be the 'great music' of the next century), but recognise that it needs careful handling and a great deal of explanation. We know from the letters we receive from all over the world (our mailing list for monthly fact sheets includes people from more than ninety countries) that WS is often the only radio station that can provide this kind of information and is much appreciated as such. (It's impossible to give an exact figure for the proportion of contemporary music that we feature in one way or another, but it's tiny – 2–3% at the most).

★   Saxophone recital – one of this year's *International Recital* concerts given by one of this country's most talented young musicians, winner of many inter-national prizes, on an instrument now taken seriously in the concert hall and for which a great deal of music is now being written.

★   Most of his other points are ones of scheduling over which I have no control, but a couple of other observations:

Whole operas? – well, we'd love to, but large amounts of space on a crowded schedule for what many consider a minority interest is difficult to find (but we do produce series about opera wherever possible with copious musical illustrations).

Series of Beethoven quartets or Haydn symphonies? – wonderful if they appeal to you but with only three hours of music programmes per week, is it fair to give over such a large proportion for such a long time to the works of one composer?

What about the vast wealth of music 'from the twelfth century up to the present time'?

To sum up: As Mr Hare rightly implies, music is a vast subject and we try very hard to reflect as much of it as possible in the little airtime that's available. The level of knowledge of our listeners varies hugely – from professors of music from as far apart as America and China, to those who know almost nothing but are eager to learn. In these circumstances, rather than provide bland music and commentary which will offend no one, we actively aim to provide thought-provoking programmes that will appeal to different levels of listeners over the period of a week's listening – it's always a tightrope act to interest one level of listener without patronising another and I am sure that we do not always succeed. And to that end we're constantly discussing, reviewing, trying to find new angles – and the views of our listeners are always a welcome aid to this process.

Jenny Bild
Executive Producer – Music

Write-On
BBC World Service
Bush House
London

Dear Nicola Barringer

After two years of hearing practically no music because Elizabeth Wright thinks we can't hear it properly on our short wave radios, suddenly we get rather a lot. There are Wagnerian sounds, and glorious Martinelli, and Bruckner for the first time since the last Proms. Some of the programmes are rather devoted to your people TALKING ABOUT music to the extent that there is little time to hear any, but it is all so much better than heretofore.

But last week some cheeky man said, 'Don't say that World Service doesn't put on music,' and announced forward the Sunday concert at 15.15 GMT. You see you have moved it forward to accommodate those time-changing people listening in America. Who else changes their clocks in the summertime? We must think of them too. We don't have to alter our time either way here. Now, your *Concert Hour*, or *Concert Hall* is too late for the Asia-Pacific region. Oceania and Japan have gone to bed; the rest of South-East Asia gets up early for Monday work so they will be in bed, as far as Burma and Bangladesh. It mast be jolly good for your musical appreciative audiences in Zanzibar, Zambia and Zaire, never mind Srebrenica.

But I heard Martinelli last night, and shall look for his CDs. And heard someone trilling again when I was wakened at 05.15 this morning. Keep it up. I sometimes think you try to fit just too much into one weekly schedule and some items could go into a fortnightly timetable.

Yours sincerely

Sam Hare

Write-On
BBC World Service
Bush House
London

17 July 1996

Dear *Write-On*

The great concern about the reorganisation of the World Service would seem to stem from the organisation itself.

Taking into consideration the effects of recent changes for the better in the layout of your programmes I feel quite confident in not interfering or trying to interfere. I wish you luck and trust to your good judgement. There must be a lot of dead wood in the building which can be got rid of.

I hope that you achieve what you set out to do. For the past several months since I last wrote I have enjoyed, for once, listening a lot to World Service without any desire to switch off. The programmes are no longer silly and annoying; they have suddenly become informative, stimulating and entertaining. What more could one want from what has to be a very varied presentation? Except of course more music. One hears little real music and *Concert Hour* or *Hall* is now beamed to Madagascar and Srebrenica. But no great matter; the listener is being treated for once as an adult.

Except for that Westminster Abbey threnody for Aids victims, which was weird, your church services have come from some of the great churches and cathedrals with proper choirs and organs. Gone are the days when we had guitar bands and hand-clapping from the Cardiff Docks. Let us hear those hymns again from 'England's pleasant land' though it may offend a tiny few Scots.

Listeners in Britain complain that 'the BBC has a lot to answer for'. Now what do they mean? Certainly the World Service has suffered when it has borrowed silly fringe attitudes and rude language plays and one wonders who is in charge – or is it a free-for-all? Vulgar abuse used to be common in some plays and much fun was made of the Royals.

So please throw out those fellow-travellers of the IRA and the Comintern and get back to common sense.

Let there be as little 'pop' music as possible but what there is should be of the best quality. The younger listener has to be attracted somehow. The high point of your broadcasting comes at 14.05 GMT on Sundays with Sheena MacDonald. That and your historical reviews which are first class.

Yours faithfully

Sam Hare

Viewer & Listener Information
British Broadcasting Corporation
Villiers House
The Broadway
Ealing
London W5 2PA

30 July 1996

Dear Mr Hare

I have been asked to thank you on behalf of the Chairman for your letter of 17 July about the World Service.

We are grateful to all those who write to us as you have done with their views. Taken with the results of our day-to-day audience research, their letters help us to keep in touch with our audiences and to plan our programmes for the future. I am pleased to note that you feel World Service programmes have improved in recent weeks.

Thank you again for contributing your views.

Yours sincerely

Ed Harris
Viewer & Listener Correspondence

World Service
International Audience Correspondence
British Broadcasting Corporation
Bush House
PO Box 76
Strand
London WC2B 4PH

9 August 1996

Dear Mr Hare

Thank you for your letter addressed to Sam Younger, the Managing Director of the World Service. As I am sure you will appreciate, the Managing Director receives a great many more letters than he can deal with personally, so once they have been read they are forwarded to this department for reply.

The current situation with regard to the BBC's new structure is as follows. Under the new structure proposed for the BBC, World Service will retain absolute control over the specifying, commissioning and scheduling of all its programmes. It will commission its English language output, other than news and current affairs, from the new BBC Production directorate or from independent producers. There will be a designated World Service news and current affairs team based in Bush House, which will provide daily programmes in English and all news services for the language services.

World Service is determined that, whatever its future structure may be, its editorial independence and the distinctiveness of its news agenda will be maintained.

The Foreign and Commonwealth Office, which administers the grant-in-aid from Parliament which funds World Service, has expressed some concern at the potential impact of the proposed changes, in particular with regard to the quality of output. It has been agreed that a joint FCO/World Service working group, involving Sam Younger, and with access to independent advice, will be set up to address that concern, and will report to the Foreign Secretary and to the Chairman of the BBC in October. Mr Younger is being kept informed of all audience reaction.

Yours sincerely

E Lindstedt

BBC World Service
Bush House
London

19 August 1996

Dear Sam Younger

The BBC had an eminent newsreader named Trevor McDonald. As listeners we are not too familiar with his face but enjoy his diction. He states that he learnt his excellent speech by listening to the BBC.

How now today?

Will your listeners abroad today now learn how to speak correct English in the same way? There is so much mispronunciation and no correction of it that the BBC is responsible for promulgating degenerate pronunciation of the language.

Of course it is fashionable to be degenerate, to disobey all rules, to accept tradition (common sense) as nonsense, not to wear evening dress to read the news, have one's cap worn back to front and go unwashed. But where should the standard be set?

Let us at least broadcast in an accepted form of English. Your critics are going to come mainly from faraway places where the people enjoy the correct use of this language and value its proper elocution. They will be amused too at the wrong sounding of their local proper nouns.

To wit:

con-TRIB-ute not con-tri-BUTE. dis-TRIB-ute not dis-tri-BUTE.

and

e-QUIV-oc-al not E-qui-VOC-al. (13 August approx.)

The pronunciation of 'controversy' is always controversial.

I don't think it is 'con-tro-VER-sy' to rhyme with Percy. Nor is it 'con-TROV-er-sy'. Fowler suggests the English 'gobble' of 'CON-tro-ver-sy' with the last three syllables swallowed. In overseas broadcasting so that the word is better understood, the American habit of equal emphasis, though incorrect, on each of the syllables would better convey the meaning and the sense. Which is what is intended in speech and communication.

I see little point in this demonstration of false egalitarianism by introducing the regional accents, except in sports programmes where it does not matter. Generally speaking, announcers should speak the speech so that all can understand. You do choose your speakers with regional accents, of course. One does not hear, ever, the north-eastern sound or the Geordie, for instance. But listeners 'abroad' will wish to hear the 'accepted English', not an accented sound coloured by the provinces, or Wales or Ireland or Scotland. Except of course for sports reports.

It has been pointed out to me that you also misuse the verb 'convince'. One may 'be convinced' in that one's convictions are changed. One can 'convince another person' and change his convictions. But one cannot 'convince someone TO DO SOMETHING'. You 'persuade them'.

That is all.

Thank you for your reply.

I have faith that the World Service will retain its merits and its demerits will decline. There is a lot of spring-cleaning to be done and I am sure economies can be made.

Yours sincerely

Sam Hare

Anything Goes
BBC World Service
Bush House
London WC2

27 January 1997

Dear Bob Holness

Many years ago, like thirty, the BBC Third Programme would have a very erudite music programme on a Sunday morning edited by Julian Herbage and Anna Instone.

A contributor to this very serious programme was Hermione Gingold, with her brief biography of the 'little known Eskimo composer' Groch or some name like that.

Could we hear this again? Unless it is too long.

Yours sincerely

Sam Hare

Elizabeth Wright
Head of Region, Asia-Pacific
Bush House
London WC2B 4PH

27 January 1997

Dear Elizabeth Wright

In the last six months since I last wrote you have managed to transform the World Service. Any economies made are not noticeable, except possibly by certain staff and hangers-on who have moved.

The programmes are excellent. All have been changed. I will criticise no more.

We don't seem to have to listen to adolescent crap or programmes that talk down to feeble minds. No more rude language plays.

That Irish bias that seemed to come with the *Manchester Guardian* contingent has been diluted. Did you locate those IRA fellow-travellers?

Though the mischief-makers have largely gone, one remains. During the advance announcement of music to come, listeners were invited to guess the composer of the background music: was it Mozart? Was it Haydn? And the music ebbed and flowed. The music was very definitely not the mid/late eighteenth-century Bohemian sound as described, but a recording of Tchaikovsky's First Piano Concerto in B Flat Minor booming out its sonorous chords! Was this an accident or some scrumptious jape by one of the chums? This was rectified by the time of the repeat announcement and we learnt the true nature of this little-known Czech composer, Van Helms or some such name.

Your church services from wherever have become a delight to listen to. Whoever was in charge of selecting them in the past was just taking the mickey out of the Church. If you wish to mock, you could always have a programme on this excess of bishops, and poncey bishops at that, stemming from the great increase in congregations of the last century. With the great diminution in this century's congregation, I see no dilution of the numbers of bishops. It's a case of all chiefs and no Indians. There have been great bishops, but not many. Bishop Hensley Henson of Durham (1920–1940) was one who spoke out and wisely too. Keep your eye on the present Dean of Durham; it was he who gave approval for *The Messenger*, that audio-visual film of a naked man emerging from a swimming pool which was shown against the West doors of Durham Cathedral last September. What a nonsense! There was no message, except perhaps that this man could stay under water for three minutes or so. No doubt it intrigued those unfamiliar with a male full frontal. It was disrespectful to sully this great church's long and noble history with trash of this kind. The Dean is the Very Reverend John Arnold. We may expect more trash from him in the future, since he is unrepentant.

Anything Sheena MacDonald presents is bound to be good and worth listening to.

There is much more music now. Well, I hear much more music. Last year I wrote several times and letters came back from Jenny Bild and others. But I must thank you. There is much more to listen to and yesterday there was even a blast of Bruckner's Eighth symphony, briefly. I have no complaints.

Andy Kershaw introduces more and more the music of all those countries we mentioned last year, and it is interesting to hear his programmes. This music is far better than that of our amateurs pretending they are playing Afro-Caribbean music when one can listen to the original beat and harmonies from Africa itself, and Madagascar, Mauritius and the Seychelles; he has no need to repeat himself with such a choice, from Mindanao to Sumatra to Ecuador.

Pronunciation of those words: contribute, distribute, equivocal, still defeats most of your people. Have you no school-ma'am who could pick them up? As Trevor McDonald has said, he learnt his excellent pronunciation by listening to the BBC years ago. You wouldn't learn to 'speak it proper' today by listening!

I have heard the 'stringers' for your present play on the monarchy. Such an easy subject and what a target. The motivation of whoever who thought it a jolly romp to tilt at Prince Charles in this way, is the old one of 'knocking authority'. Coming close to election time it might have the effect of listeners re-examining their thoughts about Prince Charles. He is no dope. He is educated with an enquiring mind. His thoughts are worth listening to, though perhaps generally the public do not quite see what he is getting at. That is the problem with someone who has an education, and maybe it was 'Rab' Butler at Cambridge who gave him this way of seeing both sides of a question at the same time. Maybe it is time for someone to show all his good points.

With a General Election looming, is it really necessary for any mention of the Labour Party, or Tony Blair, to be followed by the qualifying clause 'which is expected to form the new government after the election' or 'who is fully expected to become Prime Minister after the election'? Since both state publicly that they are not going to change the present policies of the Conservative Government, you may as well leave it where it is!

Yours sincerely

Sam Hare

World Service
British Broadcasting Corporation
Bush House
PO Box 76
Strand
London WC2B 4PH

29 January 1997

Dear Mr Hare

Thank you for your letter dated the 27 January.

I am delighted to hear that you are pleased with the programmes you listen to on World Service, but I really cannot claim any credit!

Once again, thank you for writing and for your interest in the BBC World Service.

Yours sincerely

Elizabeth Wright
Head of Region, Asia-Pacific

BBC World Service
International Audience Correspondence
British Broadcasting Corporation
Bush House
PO Box 76
Strand
London WC2B 4PH

13 February 1997

Dear Mr Hare

Thank you for writing to the Managing Director, World Service. I am sure you appreciate that Mr Younger cannot reply to each of the many letters he receives and has asked this office to reply to your letter on his behalf.

We are always interested in the feedback we receive from listeners on our output and scheduling and appreciate the time you have taken in writing to us with your views. Your comments have been circulated to the appropriate departments here at Bush House, where they will be noted.

I enclose our current programme guide for your region of the world. This guide is valid until the end of March and I shall forward you a copy of the new guide as soon as it is available.

Thank you again for your interest in the World Service.

Yours sincerely

J Allen

Enc. programme guide

Reply to J Allen

Thank you for your reply.

Though I am a regular listener at certain times, these seem to be quite the wrong times for the programmes one now misses. You must admit that there have been changes in the recent twelve months.

Too regularly one gets inflicted with *Multi-Track* This and *Multi-Track* That and *Megamix* four times and *Sports Round-Up* and *Sports Report*. These times never vary as though they have some religious quality. After 1 April I will let you know how much real music I hear.

Actually, the Programme Guide that was enclosed, for which I thank you, stops at Oman and Turkmenistan. We are further over, getting on for Hong Kong.

One can quite understand the problems involved in providing a 'World Programme' for all sorts of people, from the Primitive to the Decadent, but I did think that a 'two-and-a-half-hour band' moving on round the world as each sector wakes up would be suitable. And I note that you have chosen FIVE such streams. However, if one can only tune in on short wave then the waking hours of the morning are the ones for clearest listening, until the sun goes down.

In that 'two-and-a-half-hour band' one could try and slot in the several news bulletins, full or in brief. Then around these and the occasional *Sports Report* fit in the music, the interest talk, the interview, and each day different. Do the young have to be pandered to every day? I would have thought very occasionally would be enough or for fifteen minutes once a day. Their attention span is really very short; about fifteen seconds is often all they can allow.

Now what is politic for the UK may not be good enough for the rest of the world. One feels there is a rag-bag of 'light programmes' to pick from and the World Service gets some of them as fillers. I mean the form of speech used in plays and the very foul language. In most parts of the English-speaking world the people aim to speak English properly and 'nicely', because it helps them to get a good job and get on. This may no longer be fashionable in Britain where any common accent is approved whether it be 'Estuary English' or another. It is not accepted in the East, anyway, where they speak the language well, when they want to.

Now what sort of example is Andy Kershaw? What sort of message are you sending? That you don't care about the rest of the world? There used to be an interminable soap opera broadcast that was a vehicle for all that was wrong with Britain, the bad accents, foul and vulgar speech, bastard babies and fighting parents, situations that were topical and relevant at home, but would only be shocking and not understood abroad. Your writers love these 'challenging' themes.

It is all very well poking fun at accepted standards, but that is for home-side consumption, not abroad. Which goes also for the habitual ridicule of the monarchy and the Royal Family. 'Abroad' people don't understand this. Some time ago there was an interview with your 'resident joker' who admitted he deliberately made fun of the Royal Family and thought jokes about them were quite within the rules of British broadcasting. Surely not so. Isn't all this just the aftermath of International Communism whose intention in practice was to undermine and destabilise our recognised standards and institutions? Judging by their effect upon the Church of England, our education in schools, even the National Health Service, this communism has been very successful.

If 'tradition' can be defined as the handing on of the practices and common sense of past generations, then you are not upholding tradition at all. And you seem to take pride that the old BBC standards are being so diminished and demolished, and that you are having a hand in it.

In your *Megamix* you use this 'gutter English', maybe as a form of clevering or familiarity, and seem to condone poor behaviour. For instance you almost praise the boy who stole his father's credit card and flew to Malaysia. It was thought to be 'funny'. No one said it was wrong. *Megamix* is not very clever and has surely had its run? Gavin Claxton must be a middle-aged teenager by now and grown out of his bobby-sox. Is it of great value to you to have those listeners' letters wanting T-shirts? It will of course provide employment to a good number of people who otherwise would have nothing to do.

One detects a strong Manchester-Irish influence in the management of the BBC today. There are various lines of bias which should not be so evident, such as favouring Sinn Fein, or the ANC in South Africa. There should be no favouring.

There. That is quite enough grumbling!

Yours sincerely

Sam Hare

Mr Sam Younger
BBC World Service
Bush House
London

14 May 1997

Dear Sam Younger

I think I should have kept my big mouth shut when I last wrote to you (27 January 1997). I was full of praise for all the changes you had made. But someone has been fiddling again with the schedule.

I fully realise that you have little time between one news bulletin and the next and I wouldn't think of stopping any of those, but there seems to be less time available for Proper Music. You will find that there is just the same amount of time given to serious music, but it is just with your rearrangements I am unable to hear any of it. It has disappeared from my listening time. Now it has become scheduled for the Nicobar Islands and Bangladesh. 23.45 GMT is just too late for this Singapore listener, and Hong Kong too.

With your new schedule I hear repetitions of the same far too often. That silly woman, Mrs Miller, from the archives, I must have heard six times. How that?

Your teeny education programmes seem to be 'dumbed down' for 'Programmes for Schools'. We never used to have these and they obviously are borrowed from Home Service programmes as cheap fillers.

So where's the music gone?

Your drama is erratic. *Richard II* (or was it III) was awful, the speeches read from a bit of paper with no understanding of what the words were meaning. Thornton Wilder was excellent. Then your *Importance of Being Ernest* was atrocious. Is no one taught how to speak? All the voices sounded as though they came from *Are You Being Served?* They did not speak like that! Your drama programmes are usually so well done so long as you keep off the violent, shrieking, swearing, vulgar dialect ones that were a favourite of some producer who wished to shock.

Your church services have gone off too. It would be pleasant to revert once more to the great churches, abbeys, cathedrals of Britain and hear their services and sometimes without the chirruping of a pert child or female reading the lessons.

Sports news has not diminished. It is in the news bulletin then again fifteen minutes later in *Sports Report*! Too much.

Congratulations though on all your recent plaudits!

Yours sincerely

Sam Hare

Elizabeth Wright
Head of Region, Asia-Pacific
Bush House
London

21 June 1997

Dear Elizabeth Wright

It is time for another change in your programmes.

1. The World Service has become irritating and the intervals between those important news bulletins are becoming filled up with rubbish.

2. There is too much repetition – over, is it two weeks now? – of the same little programmes.

3. There are little fragments and scraps of trash. Where do they come from? *Children's Hour*?

4. Regularly, and for what seems an interminable time, there has been a weary Maddy Prior with *A Cappella*. This is surely for a minority audience if there was one.

5. There are those snippets of lectures and instructions over health matters. On how the British family is constructed. The interviewing of feckless females who can't give up smoking. And other feckless females as well as feckless males. There seem to be plenty about. Why do you have to soften those long and important words with a simper and some tinkety-tonk music? Most listeners can take it straight.

6. *Megamix* and *Multi-Tracks* used to be the signal to switch off. Now it is almost anything, except the news.

7. And not an atom of music. That is, proper music. For Maldives only.

8. Even the *Music Quiz* you have 'dumbed down' so as to make fun and mock those who have a knowledge of more than 'pop'. It is no longer informative, and another reason for switching off.

9. You now have a new voice and he can't pronounce his Rs. For instance 'fWom our Woving Weporter Wonald Wadford' etc. He is given too many Rs to speak. Is this deliberate, or just an accident? Was someone doing 'a funny' putting him on?

10. Certainly in broadcasting to Asian countries it might be noted that the average villager of these countries and even hilltop aboriginal tribes have more experience and traditional practices (common sense) of the upbringing of children. They form small societies of helpful and neighbourly people with obedient offspring, unlike in the Western 'developed' nations. Their civilisation and society have been in existence for some thousands of years before the West even began. The BBC Sociology Department could perhaps learn a thing or two from this 'Third' World.

11. It is odd to broadcast obviously VISUAL programmes, such as those about someone's collection of paintings, cartoons and so on. More suited to television or the cinema, yes? Whose daft idea was this? And then there is this repetition and repetition at the SAME TIMES. If one has heard it once at a certain time then MOVE the programme to a different time the next week. When it has been heard FOUR times it becomes very boring. That is bad planning on your part.

12. The Foreign Office might well listen in and monitor how their money is being spent on 'promoting Britain abroad'. Perhaps you do not feel that this is your mission? British Trade and High Commissioners and their associated British Councils all do an excellent job. Are you helping? The image of Britain today is that of the decadent seventies, slothful, resentful, dirty and ill-mannered. What sort of example is this to, say,

the Asian of almost any degree who baths twice a day and will change afterwards into clean clothes.

13. What a silly programme, or series (Good Heavens!), on *Born a Girl*. What rubbish! Listen to the one on the Island of Siros! Perhaps of course this inane and banal monologue was contrived in your Effects Department, as I suspect many programmes are; the babies crying on famine reports, the noisy rioters anywhere and so on. You must have many useful recordings.

14. Business Report. There is a Larry Moses and someone called Bob Roscoe[9] speaking on behalf of 'HSBCJAMESCAPELNEWYORK' who are quite unintelligible.

Yours sincerely

Same Hare

---

[9] Every morning one waited for this Wall Street commentator with his snarling monotone. Maybe Bronx, Queen's or Brooklyn, one would not know. Larry Moses must have been another. They seemed to speak without moving their lips or that fat cigar from them.

World Service
International Audience Correspondence
British Broadcasting Corporation
Bush House
PO Box 76
Strand
London WC2B 4PH

11 July 1997

Dear Mr Hare

Thank you for your recent letter to the Managing Director, BBC World Service.

We have forwarded a copy of your letter to the Head of Region, Asia and the Pacific and our planning and scheduling department where your various points regarding our output will be noted.

We are always interested in the feedback we receive from our listeners and appreciate the time you have taken in writing to us with your views.

Thank you for your interest in the World Service.

Yours sincerely

J Allen

Enc. programme guide

BBC World Service

Dear Sir/Madam

There seems to be so much waffle about GLOBAL
WARMING and I have read something like the enclosed
before.

One wonders who these people are with vested
interests in alarming the world when it is all so
unnecessary.

Please read and inform the others!

But that does not excuse Indonesia's burning of its
forest floorboards so that regeneration of the rainforest will
never happen again. They say they have scorched the earth
the size of France. For petty gain.

Yours faithfully

Sam Hare

Science Has Spoken: Global Warming Is a Myth
By ARTHUR B. ROBINSON AND ZACHARY W. ROBINSON

The debate over how much to cut emissions has at times been heated – but the entire enterprise is futile or worse. For there is not a shred of persuasive evidence that humans have been responsible for increasing global temperatures. What's more, carbon dioxide emissions have actually been a boon for the environment.

The myth of "global warming" starts with an accurate observation: The amount of carbon dioxide in the atmosphere is rising. It is now about 360 parts per million, vs. 290 at the beginning of the twentieth century. Reasonable estimates indicate that it may eventually rise as high as 600 parts per million. This rise probably results from human burning of coal, oil and natural gas, although this is not certain. Earth's oceans and land hold some 50 times as much carbon dioxide as is in the atmosphere, and movement between these reservoirs of carbon dioxide is poorly understood. The observed rise in atmospheric carbon dioxide does correspond with the time of human release and equals about half of the amount released.

Carbon dioxide, water and a few other substances are "greenhouse gases." Due to their physics and chemistry, they tend to admit more solar energy into the atmosphere than they allow to escape. Actually, it is not so simple as this, since these substances interact among themselves and with other aspects of the atmosphere in complex ways that are not well understood. Still, it was reasonable to hypothesize that rising atmospheric carbon dioxide levels might cause atmospheric temperatures to rise. Some predicted "global warming," which has come to mean extreme greenhouse warming of the atmosphere leading to catastrophic environmental consequences.

The global-warming hypothesis, however, is no longer tenable. Scientists have been able to test it carefully, and it does not hold up. During the past 50 years, as atmospheric carbon dioxide levels have risen, scientists have made precise measurements of atmospheric temperature. These measurements have definitively shown that major atmospheric greenhouse warming of the atmosphere is not occurring and is unlikely ever to occur.

The temperature of the atmosphere fluctuates over a wide range, the result of solar activity and other influences. During the past 3,000 years, there have been five extended periods when it was distinctly warmer than today. One of the two coldest periods, known as the Little Ice Age, occurred 300 years ago. Atmospheric temperatures have been rising from that low for the past 300 years, but remain below the 3,000-year average.

Why are temperatures rising? The first chart nearby shows temperatures during the past 250 years, relative to the mean temperature for 1951–70. The same chart shows the length of the solar magnetic cycle during the same period. Close correlation between these two parameters— the shorter the solar cycle (and hence the more active the sun), the higher the temperature—demonstrates, as do other studies, that the gradual warming since the Little Ice Age and the large fluctuations during that warming have been caused by changes in solar activity.

The highest temperatures during this period occurred in about 1940. During the past 20 years, atmospheric temperatures have actually tended to go down, as shown in the second chart, based on very reliable satellite data, which have been confirmed by measurements from weather balloons.

Consider what this means for the global-warming hypothesis. This hypothesis predicts that global temperatures will rise significantly, indeed catastrophically, if atmospheric carbon dioxide rises. Most of the increase in atmospheric carbon dioxide has occurred during the past 50 years, and the increase has continued during the past 20 years. Yet there has been no significant increase in atmospheric temperature during those 50 years, and during the 20 years with the highest carbon dioxide levels, temperatures have decreased.

In science, the ultimate test is the process of experiment. If a hypothesis fails the experimental test, it must be discarded. Therefore, the scientific method requires that the global warming hypothesis be rejected.

Why, then, is there continuing scientific interest in "global warming"? There is a field of inquiry in which scientists are using computers to try to predict the weather—even global weather over very long periods. But global weather is so complicated that current data and computer methods are insufficient to make such predictions. Although it is reasonable to hope that these methods will eventually become useful, for now computer climate models are very unreliable. The second chart shows predicted temperatures for the past 20 years, based on the computer models. It's not surprising that they should have turned out wrong—after all the weatherman still has difficulty predicting local weather even for a few days. Long-term global predictions are beyond current capabilities.

So we needn't worry about human use of hydrocarbons warming the Earth. We also needn't worry about environmental calamities, even if the current, natural warming trend continues: After all the Earth has been much warmer during the past 3,000 years without ill effects.

But we should worry about the effects of the hydrocarbon rationing being proposed at Kyoto. Hydrocarbon use has major environmental benefits. A great deal of research has shown that increases in atmospheric carbon dioxide accelerate the growth rates of plants and also permit plants to grow in drier regions. Animal life, which depends upon plants, also increases.

Standing timber in the United States has already increased by 30% since 1950. Tree-ring studies further confirm this spectacular increase in tree growth rates. It has also been found that mature Amazonian rain forests are increasing in biomass at about two tons per acre per year. A composite of 279 research studies predicts that overall plant growth rates will ultimately double as carbon dioxide increases.

Hydrocarbons are needed to feed and lift from poverty vast numbers of people across the globe. This can eventually allow all human beings to live long, prosperous, healthy, productive lives. No other single technological factor is more important to the increase in the quality, length and quantity of human life than the continued, expanded and unrationed use of the Earth's hydrocarbons, of which we have proven reserves to last more than 1,000 years. Global warming is a myth. The reality is that global poverty and death would be the result of Kyoto's rationing of hydrocarbons.

Printed in *The Asian Wall Street Journal*[10] 10 December 1997

[10] Reprinted from *The Wall Street Journal Asia* © 2008 Dow Jones & Company, Inc. All rights reserved.

Write-On
BBC World Service
Bush House
London

30 March 1998

Dear Nicola Barringer

On Sunday, 29 March 1998 just before 11.30 GMT your announcer named a programme that would 'follow in just a moment' which was followed by silence, then a click, then nothing for fifteen minutes. Not even Bow Bells! Someone had boobed. Who? The local Far Eastern Railway Station of the BBC? Or at your end? Just as suddenly this silence was interrupted by some dialogue about Che Guevara and his asthma which seemed to have no relevance to the present day. I didn't listen further to catch any apology for the break in service. It has happened thus before, and maybe even at the same time and day of the week.

One often wonders what messages you feel you are giving to the world on behalf of your sponsors, the Foreign Office.

Accidentally and certainly not on purpose, I have listened through several of your new *Westways*[11] serials. What rubbish! They are consistently awful. Who would consult any of those doctors? Do you imagine that is the way real doctors would talk and work?

Then you have allowed your in-house drama experts and enthusiasts to introduce this unintelligible accent from

---

[11] *Westways* will now be forgotten. Its jaunty signature jingle and terrible voices still jar in the memory. Just whose fertile mind thought up those many different disturbed characters and situations each with a funny accent? Surely so many feckless individuals could not exist in any one community never mind a country surgery?

some South-West Scottish region. You must be out of your tiny mind! Who in the Third World with precious little knowledge of the English language could begin to understand this gibberish. Outside the Gorbals (I imagine this is Glaswegian) who else?

Yours sincerely

Sam Hare

28 January 2002

Aliens

Dear *Write-On*

You've got aliens, haven't you? Aliens never apologise for their glitches. Like gremlins. When there is a cut there is this long silence, then Bow Bells. If you're lucky.

No apology, ever.

Then news begins. Is cut. Then *Concert Hour* instead.

A whole hour of PROPER music! When did we last have that?

It won't last. We're off to Kazakhstan next week for a 'local vocal'.

You have just said we have 'lots of classical music'. Just when and where?

Now there are a lot of 'foonny voices' coming in saying they are 'the World Service in St Petersburg, Accra, Antananarivo, Mexeeeco' and so on. Why? Aliens taken over? What happened to London and Bush House? And why have that twiddly music decorating the news?

Who is the fancypants who thinks up these ideas? Like *Top of the Hour*!

How can anyone abroad now begin to learn proper plain English from the BBC, as Trevor McDonald says he did?

The BBC World Service is meant to (1) inform (i.e. the news), (2) explain (i.e. the background to news items, and (3) educate!

It is not there to entertain!

When you do your next survey in Singapore, do try to speak to more than FOUR people!

Yours faithfully

Sam Hare

5 February 2002

BBC Gone Ga-Ga!

Dear *Write-On*

The BBC spends too much time listening and fawning to the loud-voiced minority groups and does not reflect the majority opinion.

A case of 'tail wagging dog'.

It appears to be so afraid of missing some discontented group and being found politically incorrect. All they repeat are the loud-hailing opinions of those minor groups and amplify them out of all proportion.

Where is that 'unsung symphony of that silent majority'?

It would seem that the BBC no longer merits the description of being 'British' in view of its seeming disloyalty to most British institutions. Does it even recognise what 'British' means? It barely recognises the Church of England, preferring anything but that. Nor will it give the slightest credence to the achievements of the British Empire and will decry it on every occasion. Why this dislike of England, our Royal Family, its institutions, its history?

There is a very communist republican bias which should not be displayed by such an organisation as the BBC, which should be impartial, and that it is not.

Yours faithfully

Sam Hare

23 October 2002

Programmes

Dear *Write-On*

At one time, many years ago, the World Service was admirable. Now it rarely is.

Those girls you bring in to read the interviews with various people do not sound interested in what they are reading. Their spoken voice appears very artificial and not very practised. It is quite obvious to the listener that they have not done the interviewing and are just reading, with some difficulty, from a page of script. They surely must have attributes other than their rather poor enunciation of the English language.

I have heard your reasoning. That their accented English is what you think the visiting student will hear when he/she arrives. Where? At Tilbury? But only a very very small percentage of your listeners will ever reach the shores of Britain, and likely as not will end up in Glasgow where English is a foreign tongue. More probably they will remain for ever in Ulan Bator or the Shan States speaking with your received pronunciation of a glottal stop.

Christopher Gunness is fun with his strangled, startled voice asking, 'But isn't the government [wherever] doing something?' In South-East Asia, governments don't usually do anything except pinch money from the people.

The pattern of presentation has got into a mould, hasn't it? There is a persisting pattern that seemingly cannot be broken. Smug is the word.

One can guarantee there will be sound effects, whether from your own Sound Effects Department or a recording on the spot. There is the local voice in a foreign tongue and its accented interpreter, to give local colour. There has to be the background noise, the bereaved whimpering survivor, and the grief. The old dog barking and the crunch on the gravel path.

You must now be able to call up thousands of recordings of grief from all parts of the world. You do love grief. And moods. And feelings.

'What is the mood in Indonesia at this moment?' Silly question when there are thousands of islands, mostly inhabited but some not, and a disparate population of 300 million.[12] Hardly a Chipping Sodbury enquiry!

Do your presenters actually know where Indonesia is and what it looks like? Yet in the middle of a Balinese speaking with difficulty through his real sorrow, he is cut off with a curt, 'That is all we have time for!' so that you can present some advertisement for a BBC play.

There is still no real music. There used to be, with Edward Greenfield's *Collection* and a weekly (nothing daily) proper *Concert Hour* of orchestral music by well-known composers. Yet music is a part of one's culture, as literature and poetry are. Too many complaints and you get your own back by broadcasting atonal music, by Stockhausen and Schönberg, something very modern and un-musical, or ragas from South India, one of your favourite countries.

We realise, of course, your proximity at Bush House to the India Office below. Yet you have time for talks on 'earth closets' for the Third World. It is not very long ago that they were in use in England, in the colliery and country areas. And last year, on a Sunday morning, a two-hour programme that in one part dealt with NOSE PICKING!

Who is responsible? Or are decisions hidden behind committees? Name the mischief-makers and get rid of those funny people.

---

[12] Indonesia has 13,000 islands of which 6,000 are inhabited by 250,000,000 people and still growing (2007). Difficult answer then for someone asked 'What is the mood in Indonesia?' Hence an office map might come in useful for geographical questions.

They are the elitists, the ones who introduce esoteric rubbishy subjects to startle and disturb. That attitude is all right for the Royal Court Theatre in Sloane Square but not on a public service radio station, broadcasting to the world. Is it your intention that those overseas will have a strange and distorted impression of Britain? That is very 'Left wing'.

World Service is paid for by the Foreign Office and has recently been given more money. Why and what for? What will you do with the cash? Give yourselves a rise in salaries? Startle and disturb and have programmes on toilets and dirty noses?

World Service should have a notice everywhere to say that it is there to INFORM, EXPLAIN and EDUCATE. You are not supposed to be Light Programme entertainers. Why not then bring back *Mrs Dale's Diary* and the Theatre Organ? Both were about your level, except both were clean. Maybe the *Black and White Minstrel Show*? Or would that be considered racial?

And Britain is not yet 'multiracial'. London may be and is, but not the rest of the country. Ghettoes of aliens exist in Bradford and Pontefract but the general picture is not multiracial and you shouldn't keep saying so. It gives a very wrong impression.

Your clever-clever slick answers giving per cents from surveys come from figures in a book and do not relate to reality. Just how many people really were interviewed? FOUR in Singapore! True. How many yurts in Outer Mongolia did you visit?

Britain. British? Great Britain is a geographical term as opposed to 'Little' Britain which is Brittany, the diminutive used for the place those Britons went to in France after the Romans left. Know these things.

British applies to the 'culture'. So, Caribbeans, Canadians, Kenyans and Kadazans, Penang and Hong Kong Chinese, Malays and Australians can all share this 'British' culture and will accept that they are 'British', by what they do and how they think. It isn't anything else.

There is nothing wrong with that. They themselves are proud of this heritage even if you don't wish to accept it.

It is time you grew up and threw away all those childish notions of the sixties inherited from your parents. You cannot deny English history. Read it. It is, was, essentially the history of the world for the last 400 years and you should be telling it on the World Service, because what happened was true. Before that you can learn French and Spanish history.

'Sustainable Development' was the title for that recent Johannesburg conference. Yet no one pointed out that this was just what the British Empire had been doing wherever it was. Little bits of the world were exploited for the benefit of the people living there, for their eventual inheritance. And to prevent other countries getting there first. Do not denigrate that enterprise! Just list the number of cities, railroads, roadways, universities, hospitals, ports, schools, power stations, water supplies, crops, etc. that have been founded by the British. Why can't you be proud of it all? No one was oppressed.

Slavery? Again you have got it wrong, haven't you? A church service where prayers had to be said for those slaves who had been ill-treated and sold by the Whities! Nonsense. From time immemorial Africans had sold Africans to other Africans or to Arab traders. Don't you know that? And still do! Stop being soppy! WE, not the French, the Americans, the Irish or the inhabitants of Tierra del Fuego, stopped the slave trade as it existed in the eighteenth century. Give credit where credit is due!

The British Empire was brought to a standstill during the last war when Roosevelt made Churchill promise, in 1941, in return for Lend Lease whereby we got some old-fashioned armaments, that he would disband the Empire on the cessation of all hostilities, beginning with India.[13]

---

[13] There was a misreading of the Atlantic Charter. In point of fact, though Franklin Roosevelt did not like the British Empire with its trade barriers of Imperial Preference, he was President of a Nation that also had colonies, Puerto Rico, the Philippines and Hawaii, Guam, etc. In that 1941 Charter he had it stated that

Roosevelt had an election coming up and had to make some promises to his followers, and the Empire had been a more or less closed market to American products since 1820 or so. Churchill would not have kept that promise, made under duress. But then Attlee, at the end of the war, had come to power in his place and gladly started the Independence Movement in all the Colonies. Far, far too soon as it turned out. Few were ready to take over their own countries. The infrastructure might have been there but not the local superstructure. Their education had been thin and was a mere veneer. You see today why it was all a mistake at that time to grant independence to so many of those young countries. Even America has conceded that 'the Empire' had been a benevolent institution. All those Colonies were to be given their independence in the fullness of time, when they were ready and could go it alone.

You seem to have stopped those excellent programmes of research into, for example, Middle Eastern history or the background to present-day Japan. Those were good. Now we just get trivia. About earth closets. And dirty noses.

Even the old Far Eastern Broadcasting Station for the Services was more mature than your present effort.

Take heed!

Yours faithfully

Sam Hare

---

all nations should become independent and hold elections to elect a democratic government. He did not say immediately on the cessation of hostilities because he was aware of Churchill's sensitivity about India, and the rest of the Empire. It was then the Labour Government of 1945 in Britain that began the dismantling of empire, starting with Burma in January 1948, then India later in that year. Few of those countries were ready for independence. Few had economies that did not have to be subsidised by Britain. Few had much more than an infrastructure of competence in government. Most of the African states had little. The sad result is evident today where almost all those old colonies are rife with corruption and evil ways. It was a mistake to make that change so soon. It was to come. All would in time have been brought to maturity and competence with their own leaders in charge. It had always been the intention that that would be so.

9 February 2004

'How Did You Feel?' Etc. Sloppy Editing

Dear *Write-On*

Greg Dyke has gone.

Recent reports have accused the BBC of sloppy editing which may not have occurred when Nanny Birt was in charge.

It looks as though no one has been in charge since he left and below stairs the mice and the children have been given free rein.

For example, it is detestable that interviewers are allowed, maybe encouraged, to question those parents who have lost their dear and loved ones through tragedy, to wit, when cot deaths have occurred; when an Israeli man loses his pregnant wife and unborn child on the way to hospital.

This silly and inane 'How did you feel when you had lost your whole family and grandchildren and house and dog?' That sort of thing.

Why can't you leave grief alone? It is like poking round a wound.

This is 'tabloid' reporting. And 'What is the mood, in wherever?' Silly question.

Shame on you, BBC!

Yours faithfully

Sam Hare

Dr Christopher Lawson

8 February 2004

Demotic

Dear Dr Lawson

I had to look the word up in the dictionary.

In either *The Oldie*, *The Spectator*, or *The Week*, Greg Dyke's accent was described as 'demotic'. It really means 'of the people' (from demos) or 'vulgar'.

Not much better was the man who has taken over part time, Mark Byford, who sounds as though he comes from Houghton-le-Spring or Darlington.

At least, with his 'flat As', he spoke of the BBC's role in information, explanation and education. Apart from the news there is now little else.

They have lost their way.

They should be leading, not following behind the illiterate herd and trying to gain Brownie points and more listeners from the *rakyat* with their bop-bop music and far too frequent football reports. There is no need to compete with ITV or the tabloid press.

There have been and are some good programmes. Is it *Politics* or the *Business World*? There is never any music as there used to be. How long since I recorded *Anna Bolena* from the World Service?

They do not know who their audience is.

There are literate folk in Mongolia and Tibet and the Amazon jungle who will be listening to get the proper news. What do they get as well? *Top of the Pops* and *World Football*!

Both make one switch off and go back to Mahler and Satie!

Our personal friend and neighbour, Andrew, once met the BBC man who was doing an 'audience or listeners' survey' in Singapore, or the Far East. He asked him how many people had he interviewed. The man answered, 'Four!'

Who wants 'world' football? British football maybe, in dilution and no Alan Green shouting about it either. The listeners abroad surely want to hear about what goes on in Britain, not Mali or Madagascar. People in Mali and Madagascar already know what goes on there.

'Celebrities' (sic) are interviewed but who are they? I have never heard of them and I don't suppose residents of Pekin or Harbin will have any idea either. One hears incoherent muttering sportspersons and singers in unknown thumper-thumper bands and they really have nothing to say. 'Well-ah! Yer know-ah. Ma Dad said…' etc.

Certainly the Indian announcers are clear in enunciation, but one gets the impression that the India Office, actually below stairs in Bush House, has taken over Britain and the BBC and no doubt their bedrooms too.

The BBC has become soppy, shoddy, and sloppy. One enquiry pointed to the 'shoddy' editing of that *Today* report. But there is no longer any guidance for the little poppets and shoe-shop girls they get from Bedford and Basildon to read out their interviews like ham actors reading from a script. 'Pronounciation' is surely incorrect, as is 'cortesy' instead of courtesy. 'Raybidly' for rabidly. They can't do 'distribute' or 'contribute' and always put the emphasis on the '-bute' rather than on the '-trib'. That's very 'Middle' England.

Perhaps I am pettifogging. Now we have them from Sydney and Soweto. (Sowf-Effrika.)

Yours sincerely

Sam Hare

The Interview (World Service)

Mark Byford

Dear Sir/Madam

It was interesting to hear what Mark Byford had to say about the BBC. He mentioned in passing that the BBC essentially was about information, explanation and education.

But there is not enough of that.

We hear, on the World Service, frequent news reports and there is nothing wrong there. There is, though, too much in-filling with nonsense 'Light Programme' interludes of little interest to the rest of the world.

There are literate people from Mongolia to Madagascar and Mexico who listen in for reliable information, and some education about the World. The BBC should lead, not follow.

It should stop being concerned about 'listener ratings' and competing with the other broadcasting media. It could and should set an example that other broadcasting services may follow.

For instance *World Football* cannot ever competently deal with its vast subject. Listeners abroad might really only be concerned with British football. People in Mali and Macao already know what goes on in their own lands. So there need not be repetitions of so many sports reports; briefly, once in four hours would be quite sufficient, to inform.

It has been said quite recently that BBC editing of reports has been 'shoddy'. One could add sloppy and soppy to the rest of their programmes. There is sloppy pronunciation of long words in common usage. Is there no in-house elocutionist who will correct the enunciation of 'courtesy', not 'kort-essy', and 'pronunciation' not 'pro-nounciation'? 'rabidly' not 'ray-bidly. Habitually do BBC speakers say 'contribute' and 'distribute' and 'attribute' with the emphasis on the '-bute' rather than the middle syllable. This is shoddy Midlands-speak. No one corrects or knows better.

The Ticket is a miserable low-class programme that could very easily be 'disparated'. It is a signal to switch off for the rest of the day, to go back to Mahler. *Top of the Pops* likewise. Both are in the category of being soppy. Likewise the silly *Woman's Hour* What about then a *Man's Hour*? Put *Westways* in the bin too. What a lot of nonsense! What awful hysterical people! What is it for?

BBC World Service is funded by the Foreign Office, is it not? Would you like to explain to them how these non-sense kindergarten 'babby' programmes fit into the BBC's aim to inform, explain and educate?

You should always have in your mind that your listeners are English-speaking, or English-learning and intelligent people. You will never attract the slobs of the world. They don't listen.

Because they rely on this World Service, people abroad are eager to learn more of the world beyond their own country, and particularly about Britain. Hence those resumés of World Affairs, hopefully without any bias, are valuable to them.

There should be a lot of heart-searching among your editors and producers of programmes so that they can truly say they have not introduced a little bias here and there. A little left-wing Republican slant perhaps now and then? This is mischievous. Anti-Empire? Anti-Royalty? Using a little snide emphasis on certain names? It may be recalled how, after H M Queen broadcast a message to her army in Iraq or Kuwait or wherever, that the BBC cut out the normal traditional playing of the National Anthem! Who did that?

It may also be remembered that the same occurred after the Armistice Service two or three years ago. Half of the first bar of the Anthem was heard before the rest was cut. Now who did that? On whose instructions? Do you remember? Who was in charge? Communists? It must be remembered that you are the 'British' Broadcasting Corporation and should be representing Britain, not your own feelings and failings or political inclinations. There is a very interesting story to be told and Mr Schama has been telling it on the screen: that of British history. It is the story of a country whose government developed slowly out of autocracy into what it is today. Democratic government cannot happen overnight by decree as many young countries have discovered. British history can set an example for the rest of the world to follow.

We do not hear much about it as though you are ashamed to be British. You know, its Empire just some-how happened, fell together until we had rather a lot of the world to look after, and we did it very well. Did you know that? Or do you not want to know that? People were not oppressed, and generally they were happy to feel and call themselves British. Franklin D Roosevelt, regretfully, had it all dismembered in his 1941 Atlantic Charter. And why do we have this introduction of what is termed the 'demotic' accent? You have deliberately fled from being termed 'elitist' as though it is a naughty thing to be. 'Elitist' merely refers to the 'best' part of society, that it represents the best choice. In fact, to be 'top of the class'. Is that a bad thing to be? Mark Byford kept on about the BBC being the best broadcasting system and did not seem to be ashamed of it. Then make it better! Cut out the dead wood and the fungus. Scrape off those barnacles. Why then do you deliberately go to the other end of society and select programmes from the dregs? It really is another case of childish dumbing down.

We hear these 'demotic' (vulgar) accents from South Africa, America, South Australia, and the 'flat As' of the Midlands and the North. This is not the correct 'unaccented' English which is taught in the better schools, elocution and drama classes. It is common and mischievous of you to deliberately promote them. No longer will our 'British' abroad in the ex-Colonies of the Empire learn how to speak 'proper' English by listening to the BBC. There is no excuse. One knows your answer that that is the type of English foreigners will meet when they arrive at Heathrow and elsewhere. It is not your job to pre-empt their arrival with a presumption. Visitors should hear and learn to speak English with no accent except their own.

Occasionally there is a play on a Sunday evening that can be listened to. Occasionally. The rest of the time there may be something from Ghana or Gujarat. You are not the British Council trying to form a local drama society. Forget those amateurs. There are many, many British plays that would come over well on radio, but we don't want sixth formers reading *Romeo and Juliet*. That was last year's production. *Pygmalion* was excellent except for one fault.

Where has real music gone? Once there were Saturday or Sunday evening symphony concerts or even an opera now and then. No doubt your producers have dumbed-out such as these. They are not really very intellectual so don't be frightened of them. They make pleasant listening for lots of people instead of those 'babby' dronings and thump-thump of their little drums and trumpets. Are you after the five-year-olds?

In Asia, for example, there is always a large attendance at every symphony concert or music recital. You won't know that. Most large cities have their own orchestras and the audiences are well informed and knowledgeable about the 'classical' music. They are not jungle-bunnies. But if there is any 'proper music' in any of your programmes you are careful to hide it, or then replace it with some noisy 'native' band from Tbilisi or Teheran.

Wasn't it one time a 'bagpipe rendering of Byzantine choral works'? Somewhere in the woodwork at Bush House there is a nasty mind at work. Or have you got aliens? Is there no housemaster left in charge at weekends?

Usually your Christian church services are a mockery of religion. There are still, fortunately, many cathedrals and fine churches in Britain that have traditional Sunday services for Matins and Evensong. These need no manipulation by your Clever Charlies.

Those services are what are admired worldwide, but not in atheist multicultural Bush House. We do not hear them. There is no need to try to broadcast a service for every religion in the universe. Don't be daft!

Why don't you like Alistair Cooke? He gets pushed this way and that so now he never appears where he used to. He is still a very valuable reporter of important US affairs. I suppose he is regarded as being 'elitist'. Indeed he is. One of the best. Don't you like America either? You should really not let personal bias get the better of you.

But you will always choose the lowest and the worst! It suits your standard to be with the lowest common denominator! But that lowest common denominator won't help you or contribute anything for you in the long run. He doesn't want to be informed, explained to or educated.

The Foreign Office should see this email and send the Headmaster round!

I suggest you bring a few 'elites' aboard the BBC. And readers who can speak English proper! Take off your flat caps and put ties on. Try to be 'top of the class' again!

With best regards

Sam Hare

10 February 2004

The Musical News

Dear *Write-On*

Why must we have these musical accompaniments to news bulletins? Is it to attract the kiddies? So that the news is not too hard upon their little ears?

Perhaps it is 'to give employment to the artisan' or are your artisans pushing their luck and amplifiers too much? Should not your editors insist on a little less ornamentation and decoration, or even none at all?

The news is NOT *Children's Hour*!

Yours faithfully

Sam Hare

10 February 2004

Graf Spee[14]

Dear *Write-On*

Oh! I do think you should mention the part our (the British) Royal Navy played in the sinking of the *Graf Spee*. You can't really ignore it, you know. People may have forgotten.

The Germans won't be 'offended'. Not now. Have no fear!

Three of our heroic ships and crews were involved in the chase and bottling up of that German battleship off Montevideo.

The 'tourist attraction' part will come later.

Yours faithfully

Sam Hare

---

[14] *Admiral Graf Spee*, a German pocket battleship was attacked by H M cruisers *Exeter*, *Ajax* and *Achilles* in the battle of the River Plate (Argentina/Uruguay) on 13 December 1939. The German ship retreated into Montevideo harbour and five days later scuttled herself.

10 February 2004

Future Drama

Dear *Write-On*

You announce that many plays 'from all round the world' will be broadcast in the coming months. Gawd help us! Those we have already had, and quite enough thank you, are not up to BBC standard, which is high.

Those plays from the Colonies and Empire and the great Subcontinent are maybe all right for the British Council pundits, bless their cotton socks, but they are not clever or expert enough for 'world broadcasting'. They are very much 'fourth-form' productions.

BBC Drama can be excellent. At its worst is when it wants to be 'relevant' to the everyday – *Neighbours*, *Westways* sort of thing. This ends up as a shouting match between rather irrelevant characters. Not a good example. Britain, England, has a wealth of clever drama of high quality and this is what the World listener strives to hear. No other country has this. Shaw, Sheridan, Shakespeare? You have lost the way.

You should not be trying to portray 'the World' to the world. The World wants to know about Britain. Indeed you might learn something about its achievements too. There is a lot to be proud of. Do tell Mark Byford!

Yours faithfully

Sam Hare

15 February 2004

International Recital

Dear *Write-On*

There is little real music broadcast on the World Service so why waste the available time with so much gab-gab-gab interviewing the players?

Yours faithfully

Sam Hare

16 February 2004

Excellent Play

Dear *Write-On*

What an excellent production of Galsworthy's *The Mob* over the weekend. This is BBC Drama at its best. May we have more of it?

When they did *Pygmalion* last year, I think, there was just the one fault.

To wit. When Eliza returns from her presentation to 'the Princess' or whoever and finds her two mentors smugly gloating and praising each other's efforts, she quietly asks, 'And what will become of me?' As they reply that she 'can go back to selling flowers!' Eliza does not go 'Arrrgh!' as she did at the beginning of the play. She has actually become 'a lady' and instead utters that ladylike indrawn gasp of shock, and pain in the heart. It should not have been 'Arrrrgh!'

Thank you for Galsworthy. I didn't know he had written such a play. More. More.

Yours faithfully

Sam Hare

17 February 2004

One Year Traffic Surcharge

Dear *Write-On*

In London there has been a surcharge for ONE year perhaps. Your city is not exactly the first!

There has been one in Singapore for close on twenty years! Now automated and well-accepted.

Yours faithfully

Sam Hare

17 February 2004

Glitches

Dear *Write-On*

Indeed you have gremlins.

And you have apologised for them too, which is now not your habit, as of yore.

Maybe you were in a bit of a tizzy but on 2 February at 08.30 GMT you repeated straight away the programme *Just a Minute* which you had just broadcast, except for snipping off the last few minutes so as to broadcast this silly nonsense about 'This is the BBC in Antananarivo, Addis Ababa, Antofagasta, Ashkhabad', and so on.

There was an awful lot of Bow Bells when there was an absence of transmission for as long as twenty minutes and no apology, some time in the last two weeks, usually at a weekend but perhaps at other times when I do not listen.

Last Sunday at 08.00 GMT again we were blacked out. After a session of Bow Bells we would be entertained to 'A little Strauss' music. This began and soon slowly faded into some Tchaikovsky and then gave up. They tried again. It again ended up with Tchaikovsky, or Delibes, and faded out. We tried 'piano music' which was more a twangy band than piano, however, and that ceased. Is somebody getting at your relay station at that time? What goes on at 08.00 GMT? Shift change? Aliens taking over? New boy on the block?

All the weekend there was this 'hiccup' in sound transmission, about four times a minute, which is more noticeable when there is music. What goes on in Cyprus, or is it Vietnam in your relay stations?

Give it up! You are the 'BBC in London'! Not anywhere else. It wastes time anyway.

And you have all those make-believe silly voices from wherever, probably just downstairs in Bush House, and the worst is 'This is the BBC in Sydney!' which sounds more like from the Essex marshes than Australia. Give it up!

Regards

Sam Hare

14 March 2004

World Service

Dear *Write-On*

Overheard:

'Is that the BBC, Mummy?'

'Yes, dear.'

'It doesn't sound very English, Mummy. It's such funny music!

'Yes, dear. The BBC is being a bit silly.'

'It would be better if they played some British music, wouldn't it?'

'Yes, dear. It would.'

Yours faithfully

Sam Hare

26 March 2004

East Asia Today

Dear *Write-On*

So, you are removing another successful programme that is always of interest. Perhaps you have not received enough letters concerning it but that is because it is always amusing and satisfying. I know you are 'ratings conscious'.

We have no complaints. From Burma to Japan, and Mongolia through China, Thailand, Indonesia and the Philippines, just how many letters have you received? That is a large area of English listeners you are deliberately going to neglect.

It is well stated: 'When change is not necessary, then it is necessary NOT to change!'

We shall miss Christopher Gunness's anguished squeal 'But isn't the Government doing something?' and 'What is the Government doing?' as though each government out here has Meals on Wheels or a St John Ambulance Brigade round the corner.

They haven't.

Apart from Singapore, and Kuala Lumpur sometimes, most governments do not react very effectively when there is some 'orrible accident.

You should have asked us first whether or no we liked *East Asia Today*!

Yours faithfully

Sam Hare

6 April 2004

Transmission Glitches

Dear *Write-On*

Your otherwise smooth F M relay in Singapore is interrupted every ten to thirty seconds, mainly at weekends, by these momentary glitches where a whole spoken syllable or musical note is missed. They fall into a hole. Why is this mainly at weekends? Aliens left in charge?

Yours faithfully

Sam Hare

Write-On

Dear *Write-On*

Overheard:

'Mummy? I heard that BBC man, the one with the funny accent, saying they broadcast all sorts of music from classical opera to jazz and so on. When did they do classical opera? We've never heard any, have we?'

'No, dear! A very long time, some years ago, they did it once.'

'Most of those things they put on between the news seem to be for pre-school children!'

'Yes, dear!'

'Their plays and stories seem to be all African now!'

'Yes, dear!'

'Their English is not very good, either, is it? Why do they still call it the BRITISH Broadcasting Service?'

Yours faithfully

Sam Hare

10 April 2004

Dear *Write-On*

Overheard:

'Daddy? What is the World Service for?'

'Well, dear, the British Foreign Office gives the BBC money to broadcast the news…'

'Yes, I know, Daddy! Every half hour, and the football! It's boring!'

'Then they explain things and teach people all over about World Affairs.'

'Well, I haven't learnt much, Daddy! They seem to put on a lot of silly programmes!'

Yours faithfully

Sam Hare

Write-On

10 April 2004

Dear *Write-On*

Overheard:

'Daddy? Why do we have to have all that football all the time on the BBC? And do they have to shout so much, just like a football crowd! Who's Alan Green?'

'I don't know, dear. They must think it's popular.'

'I don't think people in Mongolia or Madagascar really want to know all those scores. They would be more interested in hearing what's going on in England!'

'Yes, dear.'

Yours faithfully

Sam Hare

10 April 2004

Dear *Write-On*

Overheard:

'Mummy?'

'Yes, dear.'

'Why doesn't the BBC pronounce words properly, like we're taught at school?'

'I don't know, dear. I suppose they think they're being chummy and friendly.'

'Well, I think it's silly. Some of those ladies can't even read correctly. Can they?'

'No, dear.'

'How are foreigners then going to learn to speak English the right way?'

'I don't know, dear!'

Yours faithfully

Sam Hare

10 April 2004

Dear *Write-On*

Overheard:

    'Daddy?'

    'Yes, dear?'

    'Those plays the BBC keeps putting on are not very nice, are they? I mean the language is very vulgar, often, and there is a lot of shouting. Do they have to be like that?'

    'I don't think so, dear.'

    'Aren't there lots and lots of good English plays like the ones we do at school? Wouldn't the listeners in Mongolia and Madagascar like to hear more of those?'

    'I'm sure you're right, dear.'

    'I'd like to hear them too!'

Yours faithfully

Sam Hare

10 April 2004

Dear *Write-On*

Overheard:

'Mummy?'

'Yes, dear.'

'The BBC say they play all sorts of music but there is no proper music, is there?'

'I haven't heard any for a long time.'

'They do have a BBC Symphony Orchestra and there are lots more in England, why can't we hear some proper music?'

'I think the BBC is afraid people won't listen.'

'Well, I would listen, and I think there are lots of people all over the world who would like to hear British orchestras playing PROPER music. Those International Concerts are silly! Far too much talking.'

'Yes, dear.'

Yours faithfully

Sam Hare

Write-On

11 April 2004

Dear *Write-On*

Overheard:

'Daddy? Who was Professor Higgins?'

'Oh, he was a great character in one of Bernard Shaw's plays, *Pygmalion*. They made a musical film of it, *My Fair Lady*. To win a bet he said he could change a very Cockney flower girl, Eliza, and teach her to speak properly and have good manners, like a lady. And he won.'

'I think, Daddy, that the BBC could do with a lot of Professor Higginses!'

'I think so too!'

Yours faithfully

Sam Hare

11 April 2004

Dear *Write-On*

Overheard:

'Daddy! What does "elitist" mean?'

'Well, there are some people who look upon others who appreciate the very best in books, plays, music, and opera as "elitist". It is an admission that they don't understand or even want to understand. It's a sort of upside-down snobbery.'

'Is that why we never hear good music on the BBC? They are not "elitist" then?'

'No. They certainly are not!'

'Listening to all that football is not "elitist", is it?'

'Not at all.'

Yours faithfully

Sam Hare

11 April 2004

Dear *Write-On*

Overheard:

'Mummy? How do you spell Shostakovich?'

'Why, dear?'

'I'm writing to my friend to say how at school, in music, we listened to Shostakovich and what fun it was. Such jolly music! It really was. Why doesn't the BBC play any of his music?'

'Well, I don't suppose they would know how to spell it!'

Yours faithfully

Sam Hare

11 April 2004

Dear *Write-On*

Overheard:

'Mummy! Today at school, in music, we listened to some lovely songs by Mahler. They really were beautiful. They were sung in German but we understood a little and then we had the translations. Some were a bit sad, but the others were terribly jolly. Why don't we hear Mahler on the BBC?'

'I don't suppose they know who he is, dear!'

Yours faithfully

Sam Hare

25 April 2004

Silly Plays

Dear *Write-On*

It doesn't say much for your 'selectors' of plays.

I have heard nothing but rubbish with feckless personalities and vulgar language for the last few weeks.

One listens for the shortest time then switches off.

Yours faithfully

Sam Hare

26 April 2004

Imams

Dear *Write-On*

If imams, who could even be plumbers without any train-ing, are to be required to go to school to receive instruction, may not the BBC send its readers and announcers for education in pronunciation?

Mark Whitaker for example, in his interview with Bob Simpson, drops his aitches.

Yours faithfully

Sam Hare

29 April 2004

BBC Propaganda Machine

Dear Sir/Madam

Is the BBC in favour then of Britain saying 'Yes' in a referendum?[15]

We must check its bias and 'impartiality'.

Yours faithfully

Sam Hare

---

[15] The referendum referred to was the one promised in the General Election Manifesto on whether or not Britain should 'sign up' or try to understand the new Constitution of Europe. It did indeed seem that the BBC was siding with the Government which at the time was keen on 'joining Europe'.

Daily Telegraph Letters

29 April 2004

The New Europeans[16]

Dear Sir/Madam

Those countries about to 'join Europe' are choosing this unelected dictatorship of Brussels as an improvement on the authoritarian regimes in their past. They will have little influence. Britain hasn't.

Yours faithfully

Sam Hare

---

[16] The 'New Europeans' at that moment in time were the Polish, the Czech Republic and others.

Daily Telegraph Letters

29 April 2004

Let Down by Labour Poster

Dear Sir/Madam

'Let Down by Labour!' [17]

I suggest pictures of different concerned groups of our people waiting, at a bus stop, a train platform, school gates, hospital door, or police station, all with their knickers and trousers round their ankles.

Yours faithfully

Sam Hare

---

[17] 'Let Down by Labour' suggests that promises about this referendum were now not to be carried out. Hence the 'let-down'. It was the wording of the Opposition, the Conservative Party.

29 April 2004

Fool's Gold

Dear Sir/Madam

'Tinker, tailor, soldier, sailor,
    'Napoleon, Bismarck, Hitler, Brussels.'
    What an experience for Europe!
    Switzerland is 'in' Europe, but has kept its own independence outside the European Economic Area (EEA).
    And so should Britain.
    Please can we have our fish back?

Yours faithfully

Sam Hare

25 May 2004

British Broadcasting Service

Dear *Write-On*

How wonderful for listeners to the British Broadcasting World Service in the Caribbean, Mali, Madagascar and the Pacific Islands to hear Tibetan opera!

Would they not prefer to hear a little of something about Britain?

I know that your theme is being 'multicultural' but this is surely a case of the tail wagging the dog.

You can't ever be all things to all men.

You are paid surely by the Foreign Office to export 'British' things and opinion, not play around the world finding funny programmes that are so local as to be uninteresting to the rest of the distant world.

Tibetans are the best people to broadcast Tibetan opera, not you.

Yours faithfully

Sam Hare

14 November 2004

More Gremlins

Dear *Write-On*

Those glitches in transmission get worse.

During the Armistice Day ceremony there were three and a half long 'blanks' during Elgar's *Nimrod* lasting three and four seconds, and elsewhere.

Also towards the end of the Lord's Prayer.

Subsequently they lasted as long as TEN seconds.

What's wrong?

At one time it was due to your relay station in Cyprus.

Yours faithfully

Sam Hare

11 January 2005

Syntax, Syntax!

Dear *Write-On*

Your Commissioner for News, Anne Coe, twice in three minutes used the phrase: 'There's very few instances…'

Surely this should have been 'There are very few instances…'

Likewise this morning: 'There's millions more lots…'

This is not setting a very good example of spoken English – or don't you care, have not cared, for a long time? BBC pronunciation has been sloppy for years.

Yours faithfully

Sam Hare

6 February 2005

Sunday Plays

Dear *Write-On*

Why do you try to do the British Council's job of promoting English language plays from all parts of the Empire? Often unintelligible to even English speakers never mind those in Mongolia, Madagascar and Mozambique. The dialogue is cheap and more like that from what Nanny used to call the *Housemaid's Magazine* and not to be read. Poor example of the language. Who are the noodleheads or the one noodlehead at top table who decides on these things?

From Marlowe, through Shakespeare, Sheridan, Congreve, Shaw, Barrie, Coward, Osborne, Ayckbourn, Caryl Churchill, Pinter and Stoppard and many others we have a much better choice and examples of excellent English, British drama.

So, we don't want to hear from Australia and Canada and South Africa, the other Dominions and old Colonies just because they can write in English. It has to be good, and it isn't, yet.

Yours faithfully

Sam Hare

12 February 2005

Your Dresden Coverage on BBC Television

Dear *Write-On*

The BBC is so biased.

See what truly occurred.

BBC never wants to get the story right about Dresden and repeats too often the Russian propaganda against America after the end of the 1939–45 war.

Go to Google; enter 'The Bombing of Dresden'. Find the 'Historical Analysis of the 14–15 February 1945 bombings of Dresden.' Dresden[18] was an important target in the eyes of the Russians. It was a very important railway communications centre and would have been used had Germany transferred its Panzer forces from the Western Front to the East against Russia.

Tell the truth. Don't produce a German Professor who may not even have been there and has only read the propaganda.

Dresden AND Berlin and Leipzig.

Russia fairly demanded the disruption of these railway junctions and marshalling yards. Seven important railway routes met in that city. Dresden also had armaments,

---

[18] Hugh Lunghi will confirm, he was Lord Alanbrooke's (Chief of Imperial General Staff) interpreter at Yalta and Teheran, that it was Stalin who demanded the bombing of Dresden. Indeed, Churchill may not have then been present. The order was passed from Roosevelt through General Eisenhower as the Supreme Allied Commander to Bomber Command. British planes attacked by night and the Americans by day. The important railway junction was a legitimate target. The destruction of the city hastened the end of the war in Europe. The seven railway lines joined and passed just next to the old city with its main railway station. Blame Bismarck for laying his railway track just there. He had it planned for the movement of his armies, not for fish and milk, coal and coke as we did in England.

optical (Zeiss Ikon) and photographic industries, chemicals and cigarettes and breweries, poison gas factories, an anti-aircraft and field gun factory, factories engaged in electrical and X-ray apparatus, gears and differentials and electric gauges.

Stop reading that old propaganda. The most distorted account, one that might have become the basis of the Communist propaganda against the Allies, was prepared by two German general officers for the Historical Division, European Command (USA) in 1948. They probably multiplied the number of dead by ten for the sake of exaggeration.

Now our Exeter had only a cathedral. York had railways, and a chocolate factory on the outskirts! Let us be fair in this blaming and shaming!

Remember, Britain did not start that war!

Last week, one Auschwitz survivor suggested that we 'could have bombed the railways'. We did! Most nights.

With his permission, you might phone and check with someone who was at the Yalta Conference on 11 February 1945. He is Mr Hugh A Lunghi.

You couldn't do better than that.

Yours faithfully

Sam Hare

24 February 2005

Reference 'Roo Poo' et alia

Dear Sir/Madam

'Roo Poo as a source of paper products for China?'

Better than Roo Poo and more abundant:

A better source of paper would be from the tropical tree Albizzia falcata. It grows rapidly almost anywhere north of the equator and so would grow equally well if transplanted or seeded to the south of it, in the Northern Australian tropical fringe.

It grows quickly, thirty feet in two years and a 100 feet in ten years. In five years 50% of it is usable cellulose.

Looking like a cedar of Lebanon it has a high flat canopy that shades the bare earth below. This allows for green undergrowth to develop, even alternative crops like coffee.

With longer-growing trees mixed in that green canopy of the Northern Territories might be extended and this would surely raise its low water table.

Yours faithfully

Sam Hare

Jack Bovill
World Today

24 February 2005

IBM

Dear Mr Bovill

You should read Edwin Black's *IBM and the Holocaust.*[19]

He tells how that punched card system you spoke about was used by Germany before and during the 1939–45 war to document all those people it wanted exterminating.

The same system listed the empty railcars and trains and when the Auschwitz ovens were vacant.

It all proved very efficient.

Lost profits from the European companies involved were retrieved after the war in reparations.

Yours sincerely

Sam Hare

---

[19] IBM: International Business Machines. They are renowned for inventing the 'punched card system'. But maybe the inventor of the Pianola and its perforated rolls of piano music might have first place?

15 March 2005

NHS Doctors

Sir

It seems a strange policy to deny employment to those of one's own countrymen who are professionals returning from long experience overseas, and then encourage doctors from Africa's poor nations to come to work in Britain. The latter are more needed in their own lands.

There must be numerous examples known of Scottish, Welsh, Irish and of course English doctors with a great breadth of experience who come home and find they are denied the facility of writing a prescription even for their own family. This is so! What is this crazy country coming to?

Senior doctors, senior in years, are not daft! There is a great shortage of doctors for locum duties and in general practice. The appeal of latter as a career has been destroyed by socialist doctrine. When senior judges can go on into their nineties, their colleagues in the medical profession are discarded. By whom? By lay people administering the National Health Service. They know nothing of the abilities of these doctors. They don't even ask.

Yours faithfully

Sam Hare

19 March 2005

Opium

Dear Sir/Madam

It would seem cheap at the price to go and buy all those poppies in Afghanistan as cut-flowers! Paying maybe a little over the going rate. The grower would benefit and so their economy. In cutting out the middleman and the Generals you might get shot but you would have done a good deed. If still alive then you could similarly tackle the coca harvest in Colombia.

Why not a review of poppy-growing by BBC? Follow the little seed to flowering and then the processing of the opium and who buys it and how it gets passed on through all those sinister middlemen. It must be very cheap at their local Farmers' Market. Cheaper than Chelsea.

Spare opium could be supplied in whichever form in happy opium dens in our great cities, with coffee, cocoa and lemonade and clean needles and lots of do-gooders kindly helping those that wish to come off their addiction.

One must resist the temptation to use herbicides and destroy the fertility, such as it is, of the land for ever. One might want to grow carnations, lavender or rosemary and other herbs there.

Best regards

Sam Hare

Write-On

20 March 2005

Commonwealth Day

Dear *Write-On*

The theme was education yet the only educated voice was that of Her Majesty. The programme, apart from the excellent *National Anthem* was British Council drivel. The Malaysian entry saved the day.

Yours faithfully

Sam Hare

13 July 2005

Language on World Service

Dear *Write-On*

Please tell Helen Boaden (Head of BBC News) just to 'tell it as it is'.

World Service listeners are used to all the most foul language you can think of. In your Sunday evening plays (midday to you and on a Sunday) the nastiest words are used just for the sake of using them. They have little to do with the play or plot.

We are used to getting the 'dog-end' of all the Light Programme stuff and only now at this time of year will we hear part of the Promenade Concerts.

Let me bet that you will pick out the funny ones with Byzantine mouth organs and lute-players of Azerbaijan, the sort of 'funny' music you broadcast as a Sunday 'international' concert from St George's, Bristol. Is that a loony bin?

From the style of programmes presented you must think the World Service listener is just a beer-bellied couch-footballer with an IQ of two. The sort of baby music presented only entertains children of the age.

As for your presentation of the English language, any primary school teacher would feel ashamed. It is rough, vulgar and immature, and badly pronounced.

There should be zero tolerance once more at the BBC.

Nothing sloppy any more.

Discipline of speech and presentation of informative programmes, not necessarily all educational.

Your listeners are not morons and have high IQs otherwise they wouldn't be abroad and working out of Britain.

Where's the 'proper' music for one thing? It hasn't been played for fifteen or more years, that is as a regular part of everyday programmes.

World Service listeners want to hear British drama of which there is a very great deal; Britain is famed for it. But what do we get? We get amateurish productions from the British Council in Ghana or Nigeria.

Yours faithfully

Sam Hare

17 July 2005

Religious Broadcasts

Dear *Write-On*

The BBC World Service has a unique position in broadcasting on religion. There is no one religion that is better than another. Each has just a different appropriate attraction and speed. In its weekly talk it can show how each of the eleven main religions of the world is aiming to achieve the same moral equivalent.

This golden rule is simply expressed as 'Do unto others as you would be done by' or 'Do not do unto others that which you would not have them do unto you.'

Make that the text of your sermons in each, and repeat it, as in all good sermons, three times. It will have various but similar forms of expression.

The oldest known source of this 'ruling' was in the Mahabharata of about 3,000 BC.

Each of these main religions, Zoroastrianism, Buddhism and Zen, then Jainism, Confucianism, Islam, and Christianity, or Judaism, Hinduism, Shinto, Sikhism and Tao, has arrived at this precept, in different wording, as the end-point.

Separately in different communities in the world, they have each thought of it, and of course with quite contrasting displays of theatre. As seemed necessary, in quite separate communities in the world, some have been blatant with much iconism, or none at all with an emphasis more on simplicity and contemplation.

The problem has arisen where, for one reason or another, one process gets delayed in its development and stuck in that seemingly necessary display of religious theatre, and regards that in itself as the end-point; that elaborate recitation and memorising of whichever script; the detailing of the ritual of worship in the house of their gods, the repetition of mantra again and again and so on.

Thus the public gets a blurred vision of what it is all about. That distant ethic is forgotten in that daily performance of the 'act of worship'. The worship itself becomes more important than the moral teaching.

Your broadcasts should then demonstrate and emphasise how each of those religious scenarios is aiming for that common end, where all members of a community may live together, neither jealous nor envious, not 'coveting one's neighbour's ass, maid-servant' etc., not greedy or hateful, and without pride or gluttony. These are the old vices that must be forgotten and put aside.

Society must again learn the great virtues of Ancient Greece so that the great community of people can live in harmony, respecting each other's differences, and make a display of those common threads in its tapestry of a universal, not national or personal, morality.

No one religion then is better than another. Each has just a different speed and attraction.

Is that not so?

With best regards

Sam Hare

Write-On

16 October 2005

Poor English

Dear *Write-On*

Please try to retain the English language even though you seem to no longer believe in Britain, its history or culture.

At 02.48 GMT this Sunday morning your *Mr Ticket* presenter asked: 'What is the most happiest…?' Whatever. A double superlative? Very lower class!

Yours faithfully

Sam Hare

30 October 2005

Coming Attractions

Dear *Write-On*

There is bias there:
 Subtitled 'What turns MAN into beast?'
 I object.
 Women can be just as beastly.
 Hence retitle your subject: 'What turns a PERSON into beast?'

Yours faithfully

Sam Hare

6 November 2005

'British' World Service of the BBC

Dear *Write-On*

When they were tuning in (still turning that wireless knob in Malaysia) how would anyone know when they had found the World Service of the BBC? It would be a broadcast of African/Arab/Indian/Caribbean music introduced by speakers whose pronunciation of English is not British, but more probably Nigerian, Kenyan, Uttar Pradeshian, Trinidadian, or Irish. Then they would guess right. That is the BBC WORLD SERVICE!

The better English pronunciation comes from Israel, Russia, Australia and Germany.

True 'multiculturalism' is when those of other cultures, races, have become so assimilated into the Mother country, that they feel themselves British, and no longer speak with foreign accents or needlessly exhibit un-British ways of costume and manner.

The BBC World Service could help this 'assimilation' by under-emphasising all those differences of accent and culture. Does the India Office in Bush House perhaps exert some influence?

Yours faithfully

Sam Hare

4 February 2006

Intrusion of Sound Effects Department

Dear *Write-On*

Some manageress at your top-totty table has decided that it would be 'nice' to decorate the news bulletins. It may of course be a male, if there are any left in Bush House, but it has the feminine touch.

News bulletins are more like readings from a *House-maid's Magazine*. If there is a war on somewhere or an ambush then we get bang-bang or pop-pop gun sound-tracks accompanying the bulletin.

Was it really necessary to broadcast the sound of last year's Tsunami 'just to remind us of the tragedy', complete with screams of victims? We do know many families who were seriously affected by that wave. They need no macabre reminder.

If there is great tragedy, house or building collapse, then there have to be the squeals and wailings of mothers and children. By now your Sound Effects Department must have recordings of these wailings in most languages of the world. Any public demonstration has to be accom-panied by the sound of a shouting mob. They all sound the same so one soundtrack will do. There are those interviews with speakers in foreign languages and we have first to hear the original speaker followed by an interpreter who is specially chosen with another 'foreign accent' which is almost as unintelligible. The first speaker is allowed to go on burbling in the background as 'colour' of authenticity. We believe you that he is still there, but we don't need his interference all the time.

What is needed is clear speech that can be understood in every part of the world. Adding ornamental decorative dialects merely confuses. Speaking with English dialects is also confusing. Students coming from abroad will speak better English than some of your readers and announcers, and will hope to improve their vocabulary.

You have said before that you 'thought it would be nice' if you 'spoke with the accents the students would meet on arrival'. That was very presumptuous on your part. Some speakers are very 'regional' and vulgar in their poor pronunciation.

Enough!

With best regards

Sam Hare

4 March 2006

Dresden

Dear Sir/Madam

Why must the BBC give so much prominence and sympathetic treatment to this German film on Dresden? Our war commanders were made aware of its military importance when, in February 1945 at the Yalta Conference, Josef Stalin (not 'Bomber' Harris) demanded its destruction, to take the pressure off the Eastern Front. The order was passed from Roosevelt to Eisenhower and thus to Bomber Command. By day the US bombers and at night the British carried out their missions, very successfully.

Dresden was at the junction of seven major military railroads, designed in the previous century by Bismarck to enable his armies to get quickly to either front, West or East. Hence Dresden was a prime military target, as were Leipzig, Erfurt, Chemnitz and Berlin, all being railway junctions. There were also important optical manufacturing and small arms factories there.

At that time Germany was raining down V2 rockets on London, with no specific aim except one of indiscriminate destruction. We had no defence. Daily there were many mounting casualties. The sooner we could bring Germany to its knees the better for our people.

In war there is no time for sentiment. Have you forgotten? You were not there? Earlier in that war our ancient cities like Exeter, Canterbury, York, Winchester and Coventry had their buildings ruthlessly destroyed by German bombs. Germany had no respect for our architecture. Wittily they called them 'Baedeker Raids' because they chose their targets from that named travel book.

Only France and Italy had declared some of theirs as 'Open Cities' so that they would not be bombed!

By bombing Dresden the end of that war came sooner. After four or five years (no human rights lawyers then!), our prisoners of war came home earlier to be fed properly and many fewer Jews were transported to their deaths at Auschwitz.

Let us not shed too many tears over Dresden. The architecture can be rebuilt. It had been a beautiful city.

Now, just tell it as it was. Don't be sentimental.

Yours faithfully

Sam Hare

World Service

Short on Pips?

Dear Sir/Madam

I detect a woman's hand at work.

Whatever she might say, there is no 'cool-cha' (culture) on the World Service and no art and entertainment.

How can you illustrate art on a radio programme? We cannot see it.

There is change for the sake of change like diluting the number of 'pips' at the hour and flashing silly sound advertisements for BBC programmes which we will never listen to.

Then there is all that ridiculous musical jingling behind every announcement and the 'bang-bang' and 'pop-pop' sound effects you have introduced into battle scenes, and squeals and cries of pain whenever you think it suitable.

We know we are listening to the BBC only because of the silly affected elocution of its readers trying to sound 'working-clarse'. There are the dropped 'aitches', the 'tah-rah!' and frequent sloppy use of 'thez' meaning 'there is' when referring to a plural object.

The language in the *Play of the Week* from some outback or forward ex-Colony or member of the Commonwealth is largely badly read and incomprehensible and will certainly not be understood by would-be English listeners in Mali, Mongolia and Madagascar.

I detect a Woman at Work because they confuse intellect with culture and with being confrontational and controversial. They so like to disturb, confuse and shock.

It is possible there are more English playwrights in the English language than there are the equivalent of in other countries, yet we rarely hear our Sheridan and Shakespeare, Congreve and Marlowe, Shaw and Rattigan, and the many others. These are the writers and users of good English are they not? Or don't you know?

But let us also hear Schiller and Cervantes, Dante, Turgenev and Gogol and Pushkin.

Good music is international and all can share the listening experience of the long history of European music, perhaps even beginning with our own Elizabethan music, then early Neapolitan and German and Austrian instrumental and larger symphonic works to come later.

Few women, of course, seem to enjoy music.

Some good music should be programmed daily.

The World Service listeners would again like to hear Edward Greenfield's *Selection* and a programme on the latest recordings without too much talk. It is the music we want to listen to, not someone's fancy voice talking about it. Indeed the female touch is much in evidence, e.g. the increasing number of 'Empire' lady voices and faces now shown on BBC television news broadcasts. Are there no presentable English speakers left in Britain?

Yours faithfully

Sam Hare

Russell Finch, *Over to You*

15 April 2006

Dear Mr Finch

Your overseas correspondents must have been given a 'Standard List' of questions when interviewing the sufferers of great tragedies.

A few days ago one of your men asked of one 'How many children have you lost?'

The answer was 'Two'.

'Then how many have you got left?' he asked dispassionately as though counting beans in a bean counter.

I was waiting for the next question 'And how do you feel?' which is the usual BBC practice, or 'What is the mood?'

These are so often asked when great tragedies have befallen whole communities, each person suffering tremendous family losses. It is ghoulish and heartless.

Rather than take soundtracks of women wailing and children groaning to decorate the speech, would it not be better just to describe the scene and leave quietly?

Yours sincerely

Sam Hare

19 April 2006

Dear Sam

Thanks for writing. We'd very much like to talk about your views. When is a convenient time for one of us to telephone?

Regards

Russell Finch
Assistant Producer, *Over to You*, BBC World Service

Russell Finch, *Over to You*

19 April 2006

Dear Mr Finch

Thank you.

An eminent legal colleague has just been listening to *Over to You* and has given warning that the programme is 'a jolly' and you broadcast the actual conversation, plus those sound effects in the background.

Therefore you can cancel any idea that you will have me 'on the air'. Please do not bother to phone at any time. I have never enjoyed the sound of my own voice.

I have your email and shall continue to contribute my criticism in the usual way.

Regards

Sam Hare

19 April 2006

Dear Sam

Thank you for replying. The reason I wanted to ring was to ask you for more details of the report you referred to in your email. Do you remember when it was broadcast, the name of the programme or the subject matter? Obviously it makes the point a lot stronger if we can play some evidence. Any details you can supply would be very helpful.

Regards

Russell Finch
Assistant Producer

25 June 2006

BBC Ken Loach Interview 15 June

Dear Sir/Madam

Ken Loach's opinion on colonialism[20] would appear to be very ill-formed and quite ignorant of our history.

The misinformation he displays could quite easily be East German propaganda of the fifties or from novelettes in housemaids' magazines. He states 'Everyone knows what colonialism means. Look at French Morocco...' giving that place as an example. What an appalling generalisation! At his school he was never taught about the economic development, not 'exploitation', of colonies out of necessity for, and the liberation from oppression of, the local people thereabouts. Let him check! And you check too!

Yours faithfully

Sam Hare

---

[20] There were many forms of colonialism. The Germans were quite ruthless in Africa, particularly South-West Africa. The Belgians had their labourers chained 'neck-to-neck' in the Congo. In Spanish and Portuguese colonies there was little concern about developing an economy, or an education system. Here indeed was exploitation. France might lay down fine boulevards and build town halls and theatres, here and there, but paid little attention to creating an infrastructure with the local people. The Dutch denied that their subject peoples in their East Indies were capable of anything beyond common labour. Here lies the difference from the British Colonies where a local economy had to be devised, an educational programme organised to bring forward the local people, and a strong infrastructure built to sustain that economy with trade through its ports, cities, then universities, railways, hospitals. In the future there was to be independence and government by their own people. The great number of fine cities and institutions across the world from China, Australia, South-East Asia, India, Africa and the Americas are to be counted and not to be ashamed of. The story of Britain abroad is an honourable one. Why do the schools ignore this and teach the opposite?

14 July 2006

Your Commentary

Dear Sir/Madam

On 13 July, yesterday, just after 01.00 GMT, you made comment upon the extradition of the three British men to America.

You described them as 'rich' bankers.

Exactly on what grounds was that description made?

Was it not perhaps just from an attitude of envy for those who had made a success of their lives from someone who hadn't? You have no reason whatsoever to believe any of them had great wealth.

This is spiteful, snide reporting.

Such comment is unworthy of the BBC, but not unusual. Surely some feeling of sympathy for one's fellow countrymen in this situation would have been more appropriate, rather than the old 'them and us' position of the old 'left wing'.

Is it little wonder that MI5 necessarily had an office downstairs in Broadcasting House?

Yours faithfully

Sam Hare

15 July 2006

Repeating Taliban Propaganda

Dear BBC World Service

When, in Afghanistan, your Alistair Leafhead has no concrete evidence to confirm Taliban propaganda he should not confuse listeners by repeating it, first, ahead of what the British Commander is about to say – particularly when that British Commander then denies just what the BBC reporter has said.

You think you are being 'impartial'. You know very well that you are not. Is that priority anything but partial? It would seem evident that you are taking sides. And you side with our enemy, and the world's enemy! Against our own soldiers! They are not American ones, you know.

Or are you just doing it for dramatic effect?

The British Army provides authentic information with evidence to support it. The enemy puts out propaganda.

Can this be remembered and be a basis for your future NEWS reports? Otherwise you are just relaying GOSSIP!

Now whose side are you on?

Yours faithfully

Sam Hare

28 November 2006

Grammar, Syntax, Elocution!

Dear Sir/Madam

All in one midnight GMT news bulletin.
     'Kofi Annan's remarks IS.'

Yours faithfully

Sam Hare

World Service

19 February 2007

Shackled Ghana[21]

Dear Sir/Madam

What nonsense you do peddle! Ghana was never 'shackled'!

It was President Franklin Roosevelt, who hated the British Empire, who insisted upon its dissolution at the end of the last war, together with other empires. The French, however, maintained theirs, though a defeated country, by a sleight of hand in calling its colonies '*Départements de France*'! The Belgians just ran away, leaving the Congo to revolution and mayhem.

Ghana was 'Gold Coast Colony' from 1874 and its coast castle was built by the Danes, not the British, to hold the slaves before they, the Danes, exported them to the Americas and the Indies. The British 'liberated' the inhabitants from centuries of slavery and oppression by their own chieftains. The British did not 'exploit' the land but created economic development which benefited the whole country. There was gold there already in Ashanti. Cocoa was later introduced. The country became self-sufficient.

It was after Independence, handed to them on a golden plate, that things began to go wrong. The ministries were corrupt and money was misspent. You will remember the gold bedsteads ordered by the President's wife?

---

[21] Refer to p.109. On reading the Atlantic Charter there is no insistence, on the cessation of hostilities, for immediate independence to be given to the colonies. In fairness, Franklin Roosevelt was well aware of Winston Churchill's sensitivity about the too early dismembering of the British Empire. However, Churchill's successors in the 1945 Labour Government in Britain shared no such sentiment and did not hesitate in quickly setting about its destruction.

The country had not enough experience of government. Hence there was much overspending and now the country still qualifies for international financial and technical aid.

Please try to be less East German with your Leftie propaganda.

The same warped saga of our history is imparted to our schoolchildren.

What is your object?

Winston Churchill died some years ago!

Yours faithfully

Sam Hare

World Service

18 February 2007

The Interview, Sunday 18 February 2007

Dear Sir/Madam

Please do not engage Lyse Doucet again as an interviewer. She is far too confrontational. Not an easy bedfellow!

Lyse chirrups her words. She interrupts and speaks alongside the responses. Her Irish/Canadian (?) English is really incomprehensible to the average English listener.

No one could really take down in writing what she is saying.

It would appear that her gabbled questions, whether or not she writes them herself or else just reads out another's, are designed to trip up the one who is being interviewed – to embarrass him emotionally? (E.g. the prolonged inquisition on the deaths of his brothers.) Please send Lyse back to some trouble spot again. The whole interview was an embarrassment to listen to.

Yours faithfully

Sam Hare

Annette Mackenzie

19 February 2007

The Interview, Sunday 18 February 2007

Dear Sam Hare

Thank you for taking the time to write and I am sorry you didn't like the programme.

I can assure you that Lyse is the nicest person in the flesh and people enjoy being interviewed by her. I think her style is quite conversational so she does sometimes speak alongside the guest but I think she is always understandable to most listeners. And her questions are her own!

Try her again this weekend with the Brazilian foreign minister Celso Amorim!

All the best.

Annette MacKenzie
Producer, *The Interview*

The BBC

Dear Sir/Madam

With its very generous publicity about his whereabouts and with the common knowledge that our Middle Eastern enemies are able to kidnap members of the armed forces with impunity, will the BBC and 'The Media' give, as for one of their correspondents, as much consideration, coverage, prayers, vigils and two minutes of silence if Prince Harry were to be captured?

Better surely that the BBC and media keep silent and restrain themselves.

The media must remember that wars are not fought or hostilities arranged just for their benefit so that their correspondents, by getting right 'up to the front', can attain celebrity status. In the front line they are nothing but a nuisance and it is not the responsibility of our armed forces to get them out when they stray into trouble.

Yours faithfully

Sam Hare

World Service

18 April 2007

Dear Sir/Madam

Your newsreaders seemingly have no guidance over their pronunciation.

Take for instance the man in Abuja, Nigeria, Mr Abu Bakar.

In Asiatic Islamic countries this is pronounced AB-u BAK-ar with the emphasis on each of the first syllables.

NOT, as so many of your girls read, viz: a-BOO-bakar, which sounds silly in Eastern Asian ears and we have far more millions of AB-u BAK-ars around here than they have anywhere in Africa.

You may like to check with the Nigerian High Commission with a phone call.

Best regards

Sam Hare

Morning Email to BBC World

18 April 2007

Indeed, in Iraq it is too soon to impose a democratic form of government. In fact, democracy cannot be imposed. To make it work the impetus must come from within, from those to be governed.

When one turbulent priest or religious leader can remove a whole sector of elected members of parliament that is proof enough of immaturity and that democracy cannot yet be a practical solution for Iraq. Elected members must be above such influence and beyond the reach of those with their own special interests to promote.

From malevolent totalitarian government there should be a progress through an unpopular but benevolent autocracy encouraging that independence of thought which seeks just that democratic form of government.

National Socialism, Communism and Continental forms of colonialism each replaced earlier authoritarian monarchies and dictatorships with more severe regimes. Democracy in those countries had to wait a while. Some still take direction from their many priests.

With its emphasis on economic development, education, a universal moral code, infrastructure and independent thought, British colonialism was a healthy stage between often primitive savagery towards future independent democracy.

That slow progress was suddenly terminated, too soon, by the declaration in the 1941 Atlantic Charter that on the cessation of hostilities in the last war, colonies should become independent.

Yet Roosevelt did not demand it. The 1945 Attlee/Stafford Cripps UK government achieved this premature dissolution for their own deluded satisfaction.

In so many countries, particularly in Africa, the road towards democracy was thus mistakenly postponed.

Sam Hare

World Service

Sound Effects Department

Dear Sir/Madam

As a regular though intermittent listener to BBC news and commentaries one wonders if the Sound Effects Department has not taken over your 'production numbers'. I mean that every bit of news commentary or report now has to be decorated with some sound effect. Nothing seems to be immune from this interference.

Reports from Timor Este have the cock-a-doodle-doo of some chickens in the background. Any report from the Middle East must include bombs going off or a barrage of gunfire. A tale of woe from wherever is accompanied from your Record Department of mothers and sisters wailing at different tempos and octaves, screeching if you have a recording for each country. Maybe you can get a few local people in Bush House to provide these off-stage noises.

Yours faithfully

Sam Hare

BBC

The EU Programme on Long Life Bulbs

Dear Sir

Alexandre Dumas' 'cherchez la femme' is oft quoted. With the EU proposal to phase out all cheaper incandescent light bulbs in favour of long life bulbs one should 'cherchez les capitaux engagés', i.e. the vested interests.

The long life bulbs, the BBC tells us, are now mainly made in China for German (Osram) and Dutch (Philips) monopolies. That these 'new' light bulbs give very poor colour lighting is ignored, and that they cost six times as much, to the customer.

Yours faithfully

Sam Hare

World Service

Peter Day and His Railways

Dear Sir/Madam

This morning Peter Day not once mentioned freight on railways for which they were originally designed.

Save all those 'carbon footprints'[22] made by heavy and smelly road haulage by twelve-wheeler long-based trucks across the Continent and Britain and put their containers on the rail track, saving the number of tired drivers, pollution and traffic congestion in our cities and small towns.

Hence high speed through rail goods traffic from Inverness and Holyhead to Istanbul, to Gibraltar and St Petersburg too.

From the beginning, passengers were always regarded as 'deck cargo' and not essential for making a profit. Their fares should come down and would then truly compete with the airlines.

Yours faithfully

Sam Hare

---

[22] So much waffle about 'carbon footprints'! The more carbon in the air the greener does the world become. It is seen in the tree-rings of the cut timber. The more carbon then means there is more growth in those particular years. What has to be done is to stop deforestation in order to grow palm oil which is not necessary for the food chain. In fact it ceases to be an edible food when palm oil has been heated and treated to go into a bottle. It becomes a 'trans-fat' just like those heavy cholesterols one should avoid. These probably never leave the body and just add to obesity.

7 November 2007

Lack of Respect

Dear Sir/Madam

Three or four mornings ago, a Grenadier Guards corporal was being interviewed. The questioner was unfeeling as he asked, 'How does it feel when you lose your comrades? Eh?' In as many words.

Listen to it again.

That is the sort of 'needling of the emotions' question that you used in the past after some terrible disaster, such as, 'How many sons have you now got left?' or 'How does it feel when you have lost your home, your father and mother, pet dog, and most of your children? Eh?'

You treat our forces as though they were playing some little game all on their own just for your benefit and that of the sound effects. It is a great pity that BBC interviewers have never experienced any form of National Service.

Yours faithfully

Sam Hare

8 November 2007

Waste of Money

Dear Sir/Madam

When you are so short of money, or going to be very shortly, why 'fit out a BBC studio' in some barge in Bangladesh and cruise the waters? You have a naive girl asking leading questions and sillier ones about 'How do you know when it is going to rain?' and pertinently every time 'What is your name?' The leading questions have already put the answer into the mouths of the interviewee and then he cannot stop all his vocabulary bubbling out. I feel certain you could have done it all in your home studio with the help of Sound Effects Department (even sewing machine noises) and saved us and all the taxpayers a lot of money. They must still have recordings of the old music hall turn of 'Here comes old Roger up the gravel path'. Crunch! Crunch! Arf! Arf!

Far better to show how to make a barge out of glass fibre sections and each year when the floods come they will all just float up with the tide. That's what Noah did 10,000 years ago.

Yours faithfully

Sam Hare

20 November 2007

Dear Sir/Madam

I know you have no programme on Penang, Malaysia, but you could have. This Malaysian island's city is one of the world's many Georgetowns, founded in 1786.

The entrepreneurial Chinese and others came down from Thailand's Phuket (Junkceylan) Island and began trading from Penang (Prince of Wales' Island) at the end of the eighteenth century. When Singapore opened in 1819 so the Penangites came to Singapore.

It is full of ancient dwellings 100 and 200 years old, with rather elegant large mansions built (nineteenth century) by the wealthy Chinese having made money out of tin-mining on the mainland.

No one seems to be able to stop developers pulling down these rather fine and well, unique, pieces of architecture. A bit of BBC publicity would help. Reclamation off the coast would give more than enough land for new high-rise building.

There is to be some big meeting on 23 November when there will be a protest about 'developing' the old race course (horse racing), which goes back to the late eighteenth century and is a valuable 'open space' in the city.

The Penang Heritage Society tries its level best to counter these destructive measures but they have little money to play with. They have just managed to restore a fine eighteenth century 'Suffolk House' which again deserves more publicity and further support. It is very elegant.

Can you help?

Is it not time that we were having an FM service in Kuala Lumpur which is largely English-speaking? There was supposed to be some new station opening in the south of Thailand. Is it up and running?

With best regards

Sam Hare

BBC World Service

20 January 2008

Flawed Psychology?

Dear Sir/Madam

Is the BBC psychologically flawed? Irreparably?

In the World Service on Saturday last, borrowed from elsewhere, was a programme titled *Disgust* making enquiries into what even the youngest child found to disgust them. Apart from 'vomit', 'dogs' mess' and 'chewing-gum', which the young found 'yucky', the word 'faeces' had to be mentioned many times. This follows a programme of a year or more ago discussing 'nose-picking' or 'pica'.[23]

Are there then no real men left to curb the too-many women now in charge?

It makes one think so, since the World Service never broadcasts music. That is the 'Doh-Re-Mi-Fa' sort of music and not the Tiny Tots Top Twenty Pops Toons which are broadcast by some automatons so many times over the weekends.

Women do not seem to compose much music, though they can play well what their menfolk have written. Exceptions, of course, were the great Dame Ethyl Smyth (five operas and choral works) and possibly Marie and Sidonie Goossens, though none of their works seems to have been recorded. Three only. That's three composers only.

Instead we have dirt and no music. Psychologically flawed?

Is the BBC Sound Effects Department paid then for each 'piecework'? It would seem to be so. They would

---

[23] A craving for unnatural articles as food, e.g. soil, earthworms; also nose-picking.

191

even try to decorate a semi-colon, never mind those rush-
ing waves on the Queensland coast. They are always there.
Never quite silent.

Yours faithfully

Sam Hare

Sam Hare

RE: BBC's Flawed Psychology?

It is all run from Delhi, Islamabad & Bombay now.

Jeremy Ramsey[24]

---

[24] An old Singaporean friend.

BBC World Service

10 February 2008

No Answer to My Report on 'Glitches' on Your World Transmission

Dear Sir/Madam

Since Friday last World Service has had glitches, minor breaks in your usually smooth transmission. They are still present.

Of course, one expects that it is all on 'auto-transmission' at weekends and there is no one in charge except cowboys and Indians – maybe more of the latter, since your basement at Bush House appears to be full of them.

Do you train your Mark Coles to drop his aitches? Or do you select only those who can? His awful accent was very noticeable in contrast with the lady from the Horni-man Museum.

Can we get away from the un-tuneful Indian/Pakistani music? There is a wealth of melodious stuff from the Sey-chelles, through Madagascar, Uganda, Zimbabwe, Ghana to Mali and Senegal, then over to Brazil, Paraguay and Mexico. For example there is a never-ending production of new Mariachi music every night in the main Plaza of Mexico City, never mind in Paraguay and Mali, Zim-babwe, etc.

What happened, occurred to *Music Review*? What happened to *Morning Service*? It would today be unusual to hear a proper Morning Service according to the 'old hymn-book and *Book of Common Prayer*'. Too many of the loony Lefties have interfered with what was very acceptable.

Kong Hee Fatt Choy

Sam Hare

Email to *World Today* and BBC World

10 February 2008

It's not so easy.

English (British) Common Law took some 1,000 years to evolve, out of Common Sense and Parliamentary debate and agreement.

It was not autocratic as occurs in Europe with their Napoleonic ancestry and Roman Catholic acquiescence. Nor the 'diktat' of some imams. Likewise 'democracy' takes time to evolve.

The franchise, in its infancy in England, never covered the whole populace but only slowly became inclusive of most adults, even those imprisoned, and women from about 1920. Why then do we allow those young African countries, where the populations are largely illiterate, to cast their votes? Surely the franchise there should be restricted to property owners and the responsible literate classes?

Roosevelt has been wrongly blamed for the emancipation of the British Colonies. In the Atlantic Charter of 1941, he merely stated that the peoples of the world should choose the governments of their countries. He did not insist upon immediate and early independence for our Colonies. That was the later work of the several Trotskyite Socialists of the post-war Labour Government as they stirred up 'independence movements' in Africa and wherever. This paved the way for Africa to turn to communism and the present mayhem.

Surely the Archbishop of Canterbury is not the Head of the Anglican Church. At her Coronation Her Majesty Queen Elizabeth was so anointed.

Sam Hare

BBC World Service

21 February 2008

Accra Interview 21-02-08

Dear Sir/Madam

This morning: Rather inane question by your interviewer in Accra – 'How many mosquitoes do you have?'

Yours faithfully

Sam Hare

BBC World Service

22 February 2008

BBC Bias

Dear Sir/Madam

Bias! Blatant political bias!

Not you exactly, but your television service worldwide.

Last night we waited with bated breath for the Foreign Secretary's pending announcement about those flights into and out of any British Territory, as though he may or may not have wet his pants. ('As if it mattered which platform.')[25]

With a sudden and important interruption in the news bulletin the man was shown speaking in a not very full Parliament, and at some length so that one really did not know what was the import of his great speech. It did go on and on. Was it a statement or an apology, and for what? It could have been shorter.

'Rendition', or whatever, is not a word really in our vocabulary.

The bias came after several wordy minutes, when he had stopped talking importantly and sat down, and we wondered what he had actually said. The Opposition man, William Hague, stood up. Though one had the picture of him talking and replying, we were not allowed to hear his few words, which would have been more simply put, and more to the point, than that earlier long statement or excuse.

---

[25] This refers to 'getting the wrong end of the stick' and an old *Punch* cartoon where a lady is told that her great grandfather has been killed at Waterloo and she then says, 'Which platform?'

Instead we got a BBC spokesperson, placeman or 'expert opinion' sitting with an already well-prepared statement. He could have been made to wait.

In a democracy, you are supposed to let us hear both sides of a question. Britain is not yet the communist country you would wish.

'Rendition' – *OED*: 'The surrender of a place, garrison, possession. The surrender of a person (1649). The action of rendering (US 1858).'

Yours faithfully

Sam Hare

The Forum
BBC World Service

21 March 2008

Dear Sir/Madam

My father would very often say he was not always right but never wrong.

In China in 1989 John Simpson admits he 'got it wrong'. He could get it right this time and China might learn some lessons from history.

For some thousand years before that our Asian Empires, Mogul, Mahratta, Khmer, Han, Ming and Ching, had felt the same. That they were right. Still before that in the Middle Eastern lands, Egypt, Assyria and Persia, and the Central and South American Empires, the same might well have applied.

What was common to them all was a search for a Code of Morality that suited their society, and all societies. And each came to the same basic ethic of behaviour: Do unto others as you would have them do unto you!

All eleven of the main religions of the world, Hindu, Buddhist, Jewish, Shinto, Christian, Islam, Zoroastrian, Tao, Sikh, Jain and Confucian aspired to righteousness. Each in its separate way, using parables and myths, examples and stories from the past, had arrived at the same conclusion in regard to 'how to behave to one another'.

In their separate ways they had achieved the same common end, in theory, by different means. But they forgot and did not practise what they preached.

The 'means', that is, those different religious practices and self-interested hocus-pocus, had become more important than that common 'end'. And still does.

Hence this conflict of opinion which basically need not be there, and armed warfare continues in some parts of the world. Let there then be discussion between the varying opinions.

Western powers can and must learn some lessons from the East.

And the East (China and Tibet) today can learn from the West. For instance how in 1776 Britain lost her thirteen American States by being too autocratic in denying her citizens there the vote or representation in government, yet in 1837 retained her other North American Colonies (Canada) by giving them self-government and Dominion status under the Durham Constitution. This was based upon the Palatinate (the power of the Palace) Powers given in 1075 by William the Conqueror to Walcher the then Bishop of Durham. So he was made a Prince Bishop. He had royal authority to raise his own army and navy, mint his own coin and hold his own courts of law. He had the power of the King. The governor of Canada then was the first Earl of Durham whose advocacy of this 'Palatinate' solution was eventually accepted by the House of Lords. Canada became the first Dominion.

One learns from history. As is said, if one does not learn these lessons from history then one will have to go through the experience of them yet again.

Let there be 'jaw-jaw' as Winston Churchill said, not 'war-war'. But no Democracy yet in China!

Those distant states and provinces of China could then become Dominions with their own governors and autonomy, yet with different nationalities, a shared currency perhaps and postal services, railways, etc.

They must not make the mistake of Britain in 1776 but copy its success in 1837. First it was Canada, then Australia, New Zealand and South Africa, Ceylon. India and Pakistan followed.

Perhaps Hong Kong and Taiwan could become Chinese Dominions within a Chinese Commonwealth with their own governors, rotated every five or seven years.

Yours faithfully

Sam Hare

BBC World Service

27 March 2008

Elocution

Dear Sir/Madam

Not once but many times have I suggested that you restore your elocutionist to BBC House.

Within the last hour I am sure I heard Oliver Conway pronounce 'lingerie' as 'ling-gerry' with hard 'Gs'.

Check!

Has he never bought knickers for his wife or had them off his girlfriend?

No education in the French language perhaps? 'Lingerie' is surely or as nearly pronounced as 'long-zcher-ree'.

This in reference to the visit of the President of France and the standing together of the President's wife and H M Queen.

Oliver's remark was supposed to be his funny punch line of 'Lingerie next to Royalty'.

Ha! Ha!

Yours faithfully

Sam Hare